Mindfulness

Meditation for a Stress Free Life to Live the Present Moment With Peace and Happiness

(A Practical Guide to Decluttering Your Mind)

Cody Neal

Published by Rob Miles

© **Cody Neal**

All Rights Reserved

Mindfulness: Meditation for a Stress Free Life to Live the Present Moment With Peace and Happiness (A Practical Guide to Decluttering Your Mind)

ISBN 978-1-989990-83-4

All rights reserved. No part of this guide may be reproduced in any form without permission in writing from the publisher except in the case of brief quotations embodied in critical articles or reviews.

Legal & Disclaimer

The information contained in this book is not designed to replace or take the place of any form of medicine or professional medical advice. The information in this book has been provided for educational and entertainment purposes only.

The information contained in this book has been compiled from sources deemed reliable, and it is accurate to the best of the Author's knowledge; however, the Author cannot guarantee its accuracy and validity and cannot be held liable for any errors or omissions. Changes are periodically made to this book. You must consult your doctor or get professional medical advice before using any of the suggested remedies, techniques, or information in this book.

Upon using the information contained in this book, you agree to hold harmless the Author from and against any damages, costs, and expenses, including any legal fees potentially resulting from the application of any of the information provided by this guide. This disclaimer applies to any damages or injury caused by the use and application, whether directly or indirectly, of any advice or information presented, whether for breach of contract, tort, negligence, personal injury, criminal intent, or under any other cause of action.

You agree to accept all risks of using the information presented inside this book. You need to consult a professional medical practitioner in order to ensure you are both able and healthy enough to participate in this program.

Table of Contents

INTRODUCTION 1

CHAPTER 1: HELP! I'M SO STRESSED! 3

CHAPTER 2: MINDFULNESS AND THE MONKEY 21

CHAPTER 3: KEY BENEFITS OF MEDITATION 29

CHAPTER 4: MINDFULNESS: EXERCISES TO FOLLOW 37

CHAPTER 5: INTRODUCING COGNITIVE RESTRUCTURING 52

CHAPTER 6: HOW TO START DEVELOPING MINDFULNESS 62

CHAPTER 7: INTEGRATING MINDFULNESS INTO PHYSICAL ACTIVITIES 79

CHAPTER 8: MINDFULNESS OBSTACLES AND THEIR SOLUTIONS 86

CHAPTER 9: MINDFULNESS MEDITATION 96

CHAPTER 10: LIVING IN THE PRESENT 110

CHAPTER 11: BRIEF BUT EFFECTIVE MINDFULNESS PRACTICE 117

CHAPTER 12: THE MEANING OF THINGS 127

CHAPTER 13: MINDFULNESS TIPS & TRICKS 141

CHAPTER 14: PRACTICING BUDDHIST FAITH 155

CHAPTER 15: BOOSTING YOUR SELF-ESTEEM 179

CHAPTER 16: SELF-CONFIDENT 183

CHAPTER 17: THE USE OF MINDFULNESS IN TODAY'S WORLD.......... 194

CONCLUSION... 198

Introduction

This book contains proven steps and strategies on how to live mindfully and use mindful meditation to improve your health and your life. Mindfulness is more than just a buzz word that is making its way around the Internet. Living mindfully and using mindful meditation has a huge range of scientifically proven benefits for your physical and mental health.

In todays' fast –paced world people aren't encouraged to slow down and look at the present. They are encouraged to constantly be working harder and staying connected 24 hours a day through smart phones, tablets and other technology. But this constant state of action is killing us.

Illnesses that can be caused and worsened by stress like heart disease are occurring in record numbers while people use drugs like antidepressants in record numbers trying to force themselves to work even harder and manage more stressors like family obligations, commuting, and other challenges of daily life.

Mindfulness is the cure to today's frantic pace of life and resulting unhappiness. And it's free! Everyone can become more mindful by incorporating simple practices like meditation into their lives.

Throughout this book you will find tips for developing your own mindfulness as well as stories from other people just like you who totally transformed their lives by becoming more mindful and living life in the present instead of in the past or in the future.

Chapter 1: Help! I'm So Stressed!

In today's modern world of nonstop, go-go-go attitudes, where there are deadlines to be made, a to-do list that is getting out of hand, raising kids, paying bills, you name it, it's very easy to become stressed out. Does this sound familiar? Everyone gets stressed, everyone reaches their limit. It is a normal process, especially in modern society. But it is not so much the stress that is the issue, it is how you deal with it. Let us consider what stress is, and how we can deal with it.

Stress is typically a physical response the body takes when it believes it is under attack. The body takes what is known as the "fight or flight" mode, which then makes it release certain hormones called norepinephrine, adrenaline, and cortisol, which are what makes your body prepared for action. These hormones get pumped into through your bloodstream to be deposited in places like your muscles so you can react quickly, your brain to be able to make quick decisions, and they also can other functions of the body to stop altogether, such as digestion so that all awareness is focused on the act of fight or flight. When you are placed in a dangerous situation, or any situation where the flight or flight mode may be needed, it is considered to be a healthy form of stress on the body, one which we are born with. This form of stress has been within the human being for thousands of years, and used to the advantages of ancient civilizations, such as the caveman who needed this to avoid being eaten or to focus on hunting that mammoth, Without this form of stress, we may not survive those moments where quick action is needed, such as avoiding a car accident.

However, when our bodies enter a constant state of stress, blood flow changes and gets diverted from the brain for that fight or flight mode, and then that lowers the brain's ability to function properly. This can inhibit your ability to function normally. This can become harmful to your health if the body stays in that state for extended amounts of time. The cortisol hormone has been known to decrease libido and increase glucose and blood pressure levels when there is too much of it in the body.

The fight or flight reaction can affect your body in three separate ways when it is activated, and depending on which type of person you are, each way can have major outcomes in your life.

Fight mode: When your body enters into a stressed fight mode state, your mood changes, causing you to become aggressive or agitated toward others. This is part of the natural "fight" process of stress reactions. However, in the day to day life, this can end up affecting relationships and character negatively.

Flight mode: For others, fight may not be your initial reaction. You may be the type that avoids your stressors. You do this by removing yourself from the situation instead of facing it. This is your flight mode kicking in. In a natural disaster situation that flight mode is helpful, but in everyday life? Your natural instinct actually may lead to the stressful situation getting bigger, which then increases your stress levels as you realize the issue is not going to go away by avoiding it.

Freeze mode: This is a reaction that many do not realize is part of the "fight or flight" response. Instead of getting pumped with adrenaline to fight off the attack, or the quick decision to run, some people freeze when they are under stress. This, needless to say, does not help your stressor either, as you are unable to do anything about it.

Why is it so important to manage stress? Because as we have seen, living with constant high levels of stress puts your well-being in danger. Stress can destroy your emotional state of mind and your physical health. When you are stressed, your ability to think clearly is even impaired, and therefore you cannot take pleasure in your life. By managing your stress, you will be helping yourself to end the grasp it has on your life. This will help you to become a healthier, more useful, and more contented you. By practicing some stress management routines, your life will become more stable, with time for work, associations, recreation, and fun. And with practice, the ability to stand up to stress and challenges head-on.

Stress management takes practice, and every technique does not always work for everyone. Through trial and error, you can find the right tools for you to relieve stress. Here are a few tips on how to start ridding yourself of the stress in your life.

Identify the source

The first step is to obviously figure out what it is that is causing the stress. For some, this may be very easy to figure out because they are experiencing major life stressors such as job change, divorce, health issues, money issues, etc., chronic stress can be a little tougher to pinpoint. We tend to overlook our own feelings, thoughts, and actions, and thus not realize how much they may be affecting your stress levels. Example: you are constantly worried about deadlines, and you think the deadline is the issue when in reality, it might be your tendency to procrastinate rather than the demands of the job.

Ask yourself these questions while you are trying to self-examine yourself and find your source of stress: Do you try to reason that your stress is temporary, as in, "I have so much going on right now..."? Is stress defined by you as just a normal part of work or home life? Is it easy to blame others or events for your stress? Unless you can accept responsibility for your own actions in your levels of stress, it will remain outside of your power to manage it.

One tip some have tried is to start what is called a stress journal. This can help you figure out any regular stressors and how you deal with them. Every time you start to feel stressed, write it down in your journal. As you start keeping a log, you may notice some patterns and common issues. When you start to feel stressed some good things to write about in your entry are: what is causing your stress at the moment, and if you are not sure throw a guess or two in there; how you are feeling, emotionally and physically; how you are responding to the stressor; and what did you do to make yourself feel better.

Practice what is known as the 4 A's of stress management

Stress can be predictable or unpredictable. For the predictable stressors, like a meeting with your boss, the daily commute, or dealing with family, it is possible for you to change your situation or your reactions. To do this, you can follow the 4 A's: Avoid, Alter, Adapt, Accept.

Avoid: You can avoid unnecessary stress.

Learn to say "no." Learn your limits and stick to them so you can avoid taking on too much.

Stay away from people that stress you out. This can be a tough one, especially if they are family, but if there is someone that regularly causes you stress, limit your association or end the relationship completely.

Control what is around you: If traffic bothers you, try an alternate route that has less traffic, even if it may make the commute longer, if the news bothers you, turn the channel or turn off the TV, or if shopping is something you hate, ask someone else to help or shop online. Remove the issues around you that cause stress.

Simplify your to-do list: Take a look at your schedule and daily tasks. Do you have too much on your plate? Simplify it. Move less important things to the bottom of the list, or even better, get rid of them completely.

Alter your situation: Learn to find ways to think differently

Start talking about your feelings, do not hold them inside. If there is something that is bothering you, say it. If left to sit in your mind, it can fester, and that can lead to all sorts of stress and negative emotions.

Compromise: If you think someone else's behavior is the reason for your stress, and you ask them to change, you should be willing to change yourself. Finding middle ground is always healthier and will eliminate stress

Balance your schedule: Burnout, the dreaded word of the working class. Try to find some downtime, put family life, social pursuits and even alone time as a priority to help balance your work and personal life.

Adapt to what stresses you: If you can't fix the stressor then change how you deal with it

Rethink problems: View a stressful situation in a more positive light.

The bigger picture: Look at the stressful situation and ask yourself, how important is it really? Will it matter in a week? A month? A year? If you can answer no, then ignore it and focus on something more important

Change your standards: This one can be tough for some people. Perfectionism is a huge source of stress that is completely avoidable. Stop setting your standards so high so that you can actually meet some goals and expectations.

Exercise

Exercise is one the best cures for stress. But when you are stressed it usually is the last thing you feel like doing. When you are stressed you can be in physical pain, tight shoulders, stiff neck, jaw muscles ache, migraines. Sound familiar? Of course, exercise does not sound fun. However, it is actually crucial to relieving that tension. Exercise makes your body release endorphins, and they make you feel good. Exercise can also help distract you from your daily stressors. The general recommendation is 30 minutes or more of exercise daily, you do not have to be an athlete or gym-o-holic who gets up at 4 am to go run 10 miles, any form of physical activity is beneficial, especially if you are just starting out. The point is to get up and get moving.

Simple activities to start with:

Play a movement-based video game with your kids, like tennis or dancing

Park a little farther away from the store or your office

Walk the dog

Good music to dance to

Try walking or bicycling to work or the store

Take the stairs instead of the elevator

Find someone else who wants to exercise and make it a fun partnership

Schedule some time for relaxation

So far we have discussed ways to take charge and keep a positive attitude, but getting downtime is also crucial to stress management. Living in the nonstop world we do, it can be easy to forget to take care of yourself and your needs. Making that time for relaxation will help you find that happy place where you will be able to take on life's stressors a little better.

Set your leisure time: You should try for this daily. This is the chance to unplug and take a break from all your obligations, so do not let other responsibilities get in the way.

What do you enjoy? Do it every day. Your resting activities should be something you actually like doing, even if it is just staring out at the stars at night, make sure that is what you find the time to do.

Laugh at yourself: Laughter is very therapeutic, and a sense of humor can help fight stress

Talk to someone

When you are stressed, thoughts and feelings become all one big jumble inside you. Talking it out can help to alleviate some of those bothersome feelings.

Stress can cloud your ability to think clearly, so talking things out can be very helpful

A trusted friend or your spouse can lend an ear, and may even have some helpful answers for you.

Sometimes just saying what is bothering out loud can help relieve the stress, because as you say it, you may just realize how silly that matter is.

Don't keep things bottled up if there is a repetitive thought of feelings that just won't go away, talk to someone. It can help relieve a lot of stress.

Time Management

When you stretch yourself too thin, you can get stressed because it is hard to stay on top of things, and you are unable to stay calm and focused. When you overbook yourself, you also are unable to get the time you need to feel better, such as your leisure time and a good night's sleep.

Don't over commit yourself. Don't schedule things back to back or fit it all into one day. It never works and will cause more stress than if you had done it on separate days.

Prioritize: Take a look at what to do list and pick the ones that must get done, and put the rest in order of importance.

Let others help: It is ok to ask for help and let others assist you. Trying to do everything yourself whether it is at home or at work can be a huge cause of stress. Stop trying to control it all and give tasks to others.

Have a healthy lifestyle

Besides exercise, there are other things you can do for yourself to be healthy and help minimize your stress levels.

Eat healthier: Be aware of what you eat. Eat a good breakfast so that you can focus throughout the day, and eat regular balanced meals.

Limit caffeine and sugar: Caffeine is an upper, and sugar can give you a nice boost of energy as well, however, once those highs wear off, it can cause that crashing sensation we all hate so much. By limiting the amounts you eat, you won't get those crashes and will feel better

Limit alcohol: When you are stressed it is easy to want to turn to alcohol and natural remedy to help you relax and not feel so edgy. However, this is only a temporary relief, and it only serves to hide your real issues.

Sleep: A good night's sleep is crucial to maintaining a healthy lifestyle but also to reduce stress. Your body needs that time to recharge and reset for the next day

Dealing with stress is never easy, and there is never one easy way to rid yourself of it. Life still has to go on each day, and with it will bring its own new doses of stress. But with practice and maintaining some healthy habits, you can manage your stress levels. You might even eliminate some all together! There are other techniques for managing stress as well, as well as a whole mindset that you can achieve with practice. It is called Mindfulness. What is it? The next chapter will discuss what Mindfulness is as well as how you can start to practice it.

Chapter 2: Mindfulness And The Monkey

As stated before, stress, anxiety, and fear are the enemies of peace, tranquility, and focus. It is not possible for your brain to focus when your body is experiencing stress. Fortunately, there is a solution.

What is Mindfulness?

According to Merriam-Webster, the definition is as follows:

1. The quality or state of being mindful;

2. The practice of maintaining a nonjudgmental state of heightened or complete awareness of one's thoughts,

emotions, or experiences on a moment-to-moment basis.

The second definition, though accurate, is also part of the reason mindfulness is misunderstood. Being constantly aware of your moment-to-moment experience is not achievable, except perhaps when the Buddha achieved Nirvana. For us mere regular folk, being constantly aware of your moment-to-moment experience is an ideal that you will learn to get closer to.

Even though mindfulness does involve finding ways to stay in the present moment, it does not require practitioners to be thinking in a constant stream-of-consciousness about everything they experience. A more helpful way to define mindfulness might be this:

Being aware of your thoughts, emotions, and physical senses as they are with no judgment.

If that still feels too complicated, an even simpler definition might be:

Paying attention.

It really is that simple. A person who is consumed with stress, anxiety, and regret is not capable of paying attention. When you are anticipating or rehearsing for things that may or may not happen in the future, you are not paying any attention to what is happening in your life in the present. The same goes for looking toward the past with regret. Mindfulness is paying attention to the present with openness and curiosity and accepting things as they are.

Examples of Mindful Practices

No matter your age, sex, or intelligence, you can train your brain to be mindful. Here are some examples, all of which we will talk about in detail in the next chapter:

■ Mindful breathing. Mindful breathing is a very simple way to calm feelings of stress, anxiety, and regret and center yourself in the present moment. Research tells us that those of us with slow measured breaths are calmer and happier. There are several techniques you can use to breathe mindfully.

■ Mindful eating. Many of us eat on the run, wolfing down our food and barely tasting it. We eat in our cars or at our desks at work. Mindful eating is a way of reconnecting with the food you eat in a meaningful way.

■ Mindful walking. Mindful walking is a form of meditation, and it can be applied to other physical activities as well. When we walk, we often let our minds wander and we end up feeding anxiety and regret. Walking, thinking only of each step, allows us to enjoy the walk for what it is, keeping our minds in the present.

■ Meditation. Meditation is probably the mindfulness practice that is the most widely known, and the most misunderstood. We will talk about it more in the next section of this chapter.

The most important thing you need to know about mindfulness is that it is a skill. Just as you can teach yourself how to draw a bird or sing a song, you can teach yourself how to live in a mindful way.

Meditation: What It is and is Not

Meditation is something that is frequently misunderstood. It is not religious, there is not just one way of doing it right, and it is not clearing your mind of thought. It is not done incorrectly when your mind wanders and you do not have to contort your legs into the lotus position.

Many people who meditate do so to actively pay attention to their thoughts, emotions, and physical senses for a predetermined amount of time. It helps them cope with negative emotions in a calm and effective way. Although some people may think about God or religion while they meditate, many of them do not.

Meditation is a practice. It provides concrete, observable benefits to the brain. One of the things that neuroscientists have learned in recent years is that the human brain has a remarkable ability to rewire itself (technically known as neuroplasticity). So, no matter how much we believe we cannot change our thought processes, scientific evidence has shown mindfulness and meditation practice will physiologically change your brain to think in a more calm and focused manner.

How Mindfulness Can Calm the Monkey

A brain that is pumped full of stress hormones and predisposed to scattered thoughts is the monkey swinging from tree to tree. It is incapable of sitting still. It revisits the same, unproductive pathways over and over again. It looks back at the past with regret. It looks forward to the future with anxiety.

When you practice mindfulness, you train your monkey mind. You teach it that there is another way to cope with negative emotions. Instead of swinging wildly from place to place, it has the option of sitting quietly. It has the option of giving its full attention to what is happening right now. It does not have to open the door to anxiety and regret.

The next chapter will give you the specific tools you need to calm your monkey brain and teach it a new and more productive way to cope with stress. In just 21 days, you can learn how to minimize the negative effects of stress and find a new way of living in the present.

Chapter 3: Key Benefits Of Meditation

Meditation was barely recognized by Westerners until an Indian yoga teacher named Maharishi Mahesh Yogi introduced Transcendental Meditation (TM) to the United States in 1959. The meditation presented by Maharishi to Americans used a mantra that helped to stimulate relaxation and transcend conventional thinking.

The Beatles, who studied with Maharishi in India, were a big influence on the growing popularity of meditation through the 1960s. With his popularity, Maharishi continued to train more than forty thousand meditation teachers for the next fifty years. The teachers who trained directly under Maharishi then spread out and taught the transcendental meditation technique to more than five million people around the world.

During the last part of the 20th century, other methods of meditation began to gain recognition in the West. One of these new forms of meditation was called insight or mindfulness meditation.

Mindfulness meditation aims to help a person become deeply aware of the present moment in order to be able to completely live through the here and now.

Other forms of meditation utilize visualization and guided imagery through mental pictures to promote relaxation of both mind and body. Currently, over 20 million Americans, which comprise almost 10% of the population, perform regular meditation.

Their purpose for practicing meditation ranges from managing high blood pressure, stress, anxiety, and their overall state of mind in order to live better.

The Amazing Benefits of Meditation

Nowadays, more and more health practitioners recommend meditation to resolve both mental and physical problems. Even small practices of meditation can cause major neurological improvements. A research published in Psychological Science evaluated the effects of meditation on brain wave activity. It was observed that after seven hours of meditation practice, participants showed an improvement in brain wave activity. Since the improvement was in the left frontal area, it could be easily linked to positive mood changes. Some other benefits of meditation are discussed below. Read on.

Improved Memory

Constant meditation practice has a tremendous effect on memory function.

A research conducted by Thomas Jefferson University Hospital involved fifteen senior patients suffering from Alzheimer's disease. While some participants were engaged in twelve minutes of meditation exercises on a daily basis for eight weeks, the remaining participants listened to classical music. On examining the brain scans of both the participant'sgroups, it was discovered that the people involved in meditation showed increased blood flow in different parts of the brain. Moreover, the same group felt less anxiety, better memory, and had improved memory recall.

Pain Relief

Numerous medical studies support the implementation of meditation to reduce pain. According to a study published in the Journal of Neuroscience, fifteen adults without any prior experience of meditation joined a research group. They were taught focused attention, a popular meditation style, in four sessions of 20 minutes each. A special kind of magnetic resonance imaging technique was used to scan every participant's brain activity before and after the research. While being scanned, a tiny heat producing system was attached to the body of each participant to trigger a small pain response

Stronger Immune System

A journal named Psychosomatic Medicine published the effects of meditation of the immune system's response. For the purpose of research, analysts administered a vaccine for influenza to a group of people who don't meditate as well as to those who had been engaged in meditation for the period of eight weeks.

Physiological Advantages

The mind-body advantages of meditation are as varied as its practices. Here are a few common advantages that you should know about:

Quiet meditation stabilizes your heart rate.

Moderately hypertensive people can control their blood pressure levels using meditation.

Quicker and better recovery from anxiety and the associated health issues.

Significant improvement in alpha rhythms. Alpha rhythms are high-amplitude; slow brain waves that are highly correlated with relaxation.

Meditation improves synchronization of the left and right hemispheres of the brain. This synchronization is correlated with creativity.

Meditation lowers cholesterol levels.

It reduces your requirement for oxygen and thus decreases your overall energy consumption.

Meditation ensures slower, deeper breathing.

It helps your muscles relax.

It causes a significant decrease in pain intensity.

Psychological Advantages

Physical or physiological benefits are not the only ones that you can expect to get from meditation. It also offers a plethora of psychological benefits that help you live a peaceful and of course happy life. Here are a few common effects of meditation on your psychology or mental state.

Meditation can provide you with more peace of mind and happiness.

It can help you become an empathetic person.

It can help you become a highly creative individual.

Self-actualization is another great advantage of meditation.

It causes a great reduction in both chronic and acute anxiety.

Meditation complements psychotherapy and many other approaches to treating addiction.

Chapter 4: Mindfulness: Exercises To Follow

There are thousands of resources that would tell you how to be in the moment. There are even more resources that can tell you of exercises to practice mindfulness. But how do you know which ones to follow, and which ones to ignore? How can you tell the effective ones from the others, and the ones that would help you better than the others?

In this eBook on Mindfulness, this chapter is dedicated to point out the most effective and proven mindfulness exercises that you can adopt into your lifestyle with the most ease.

One-Minute Mini Mindfulness

This is a mini exercise that can be practiced anytime, anywhere, while in any situation - sitting, standing up or lying down. You can even try this exercise right now, after reading the whole description, right in this chapter, just by following the steps mentioned below.

Take a note of the time from a watch or a clock.

The exercise will only take the next 60 seconds of your life, and nothing more.

Starting right now, focus your whole attention to your breathing.

Breath in and out for one whole minutes, as normally as you can.

Breathe in, and try to hold your breath for 6 seconds or 6 counts; then breathe out as slowly as possible.

Focus on nothing else but your breathing the whole time. Literally, try to visualize yourself breathing - the simple yet complicated process of drawing in air into your system and letting it go out again.

Repeat for around 60 seconds, which would be a total of around 6 breathe-in-breath-out cycles.

Breathe again normally and look for indications of how you are feeling.

9 out of 10 people will feel surprisingly refreshed after this simple exercise. This is because for one whole minute, you have let go of all the cares in this world - all the worries and all the troubles - to give yourself a much needed break. You have not thought of the big exam tomorrow, or worried about an ailment, or an upcoming promotion, but instead have just completely concentrated on yourself and your breathing, forsaking everything else.

The first few times, you may find your concentration slacking away, caught in some sound nearby, or someone talking. If that happens, don't lose focus but just discard these distractions and come back to yourself. If you find your mind drifting away to make plans of its own, calmly guide them back - without much struggle, but strongly.

Slowly, over time, your mind will be used to this exercise and you will be able to take this 1-minute break anytime and anywhere you feel the need, without any special preparation or environment.

Mindful Concentration

This is a similar technique which requires your complete concentration for around one to two minutes. This exercise guarantees to reintroduce yourself to the beauty of your surroundings, especially to the beautiful objects found in nature around us - some things that we usually miss out on in our hectic lives.

In this exercise, choose a natural object to focus on in your surroundings. This could be a flower on your desk, an insect that is sitting idly near you, a plant or a tree, or just the clouds in the sky. You can settle on an non-animate object too if there are nothing natural around you, but the technique works the best if it is natural.

Pick an object and look at it, concentrating on it as if you are seeing it for the first time. Even if it is something as simple as a rose, or a plant that you see every day, look at it as if you are a toddler looking at a bright toy for the first time. Look at the vibrant coloring, the texture and it's movement. Think about that object - look closely at how it is interacting with the world, or with you.

Think about the object as it is at that particular moment; don't try to imagine its roots, or history or place it in any other environment. Don't imagine the rose as it would look in your bedroom, or if that insect would fly off to another desk in the next moment. Think of this situation as a still moment in time, and concentrate without going over the other details of time and space.

For the next one or two minutes, that object should be the center of your universe, and all that you have. Don't let your concentration be guided to anything else, or any other thought. You don't have to note the time, or use an alarm clock, but just focus on it for enough that you don't get bored or other people get suspicious of your actions.

After you are done concentrating, close your eyes for a few seconds, take 1/2 deep breaths and join the rest of the world. You will feel refreshed, calm and strangely at ease with the moment that you are in.

Counting Mindfulness

This mindfulness technique requires you to count, as simple as count from 1 to 10. Did we say simple? It is actually a very hard thing to do!

You might be saying, "What could be more natural and easier than counting from one to ten? Even toddlers can do it, then why can't we?"

The trick is not to just count from 1 to 10, but to completely concentrate on it while doing the countdown. This is something that adults can do in their sleep, because we are so used to these simple countdowns that rarely does our brain concentrate only on that. When we are counting, we are actually thinking of a thousand other things at the same time. Usually, it goes like:

"Ten ... nine ... eight ... I need to make sure I take the umbrella to work ... oops!!"

"... eight ... seven ... six ... I really can't forget the water the plants today ... five ..."

" ... five ... four ... I wonder what time it is already ... two ... no, three ... two ..."

"... three ... two ... I'm concentrating as hard as I can ... one ... zero!"

You have successfully counted from ten to one, but have you been able to concentrate on it completely?

This is not what concentration looks like. While you are concentrating on your counting, the ten numbers that you are repeating in your mind should be the only thing that is on your mind at that moment.

Close your eyes, and take a deep breath. Then, as your mind is clear of all thoughts and emotions, start your counting: ten...nine...eight...three...two...one...zero.
When you reach the end, take another deep breath, and start again. Do this for as long as you need to feel relaxed, or for as long as you need to become completely focused.

If you find your mind looking for distractions while you are in the middle of a countdown, stop where you are. Take a moment to discard that thought gently, take a breath, and start again. Do this as many times as you need if you get distracted again and again. Don't be too hard on yourself if you can't concentrate from the beginning. It will come to you when you are ready.

Mindful Listening

Do you know the difference between 'hearing' something and 'listening' to it? There is a subtle but an important difference between the two concepts that we rarely ever pay attention to.

'Hearing' something is when the sounds enter our ears; we may hear the traffic, but do we really stop to think what is making all the hubbub out there? Do we try to count the numbers of cars in the road by the sound that we are making, or imagine what type of people are talking in such loud tones? No! We hear these sounds but they don't really enter our understanding or our concentration.

When we do try to comprehend what is going on, we are 'listening' to these sounds. We are trying to identify the singer by listening to a song, we are trying to know what the teacher is saying by listening to their words. Our minds may divert along the way, but still we try and concentrate on listening as well as we can.

With mindfulness, we can take the concept of 'listening' a step forward. With this particular exercise, we will not only listen and concentrate, but we will make what we are listening to our only and most important focus during this routine.

Pick something to listen to; it could be anything from your favorite song to a bird chirping away. It could be sound of the washing machine, or a vacuum cleaner if you are comfortable with it. Now, listen to it. What is there to listen to a song you have heard a thousand times before, a bird or a washing machine - you ask? Everything!

There is hidden sounds and magic in even the most common and familiar objects. Pick any one of the instruments being played in that song, and try to follow it. Imagine the tune coming out of that instrument as someone plays it. Literally, try to imagine the tune as a solid object and how it modifies and fits the rest of the instruments. Listen to the lyrics, and try to think about them. See how the music vibrates at times, and how the singer emphasizes on a single word, or how they fit the words to the tunes.

You can do almost the same with any sound that you choose - the sound of rain falling, of traffic, or birds or of the engines growling in your car.

Action Mindfulness

From the moment that we wake up in the morning to the moment that we go to bed, there are a thousand actions that we are performing automatically, without even thinking about them. Have you thought of the innumerable actions that your hand

and your brain is performing when you are doing something as simple as pouring out a glass of water, or making your bed?

While we are doing these actions that we have done at least a thousand times before, we work automatically. Our hands are doing the work while we are busy thinking of something else, something more important. This is possibly the reason why we sometimes make the mistakes that we make in these simple procedures, like lose our keys after carelessly discarding it somewhere, place the TV remote inside the fridge instead of the water bottle as we have intended to.

These things have happened to you, haven't they? They happen to everyone.

Try and put your mind into these small actions and you will be surprised to see just how much your hands and your mind has to go through to complete them.

While you are doing something as easy as making coffee, stop and regard each step carefully. See how your eyes are locating the coffee and the milk container from a number of other jars around. See how they pulled out an empty cup, reached for a spoon. Follow each step and see how you are slowly measuring the ingredients into the cup and topping it up with warm water. Now watch as your hands stir the water, turning the ingredients into a cup of steaming coffee.

All these actions, performed within a minute - and you have been doing them forever, while talking on the phone, humming to yourself or thinking about something else more important. Do you feel a little surprised at all the work you just did without even concentrating on it?

Try this technique with almost everything that you do all day - brushing your teeth, turning on the laptop at work, packing your bags, and you will feel that you can concentrate on them without thinking about other things and getting distracted all the time.

All of the techniques and exercises above has one thing in common. Can you guess what that is?

None of the exercises tells you to take time out of your busy schedule to do something dramatic, drastic or time-consuming. Rather, they are all simple and brief practices that you can implement anytime and anywhere in your life with the greatest of ease, to concentrate on the ordinary actions that you perform every day.

Chapter 5: Introducing Cognitive Restructuring

Mindfulness and cognitive restructuring go together like chutney and cheese. In CBT, mindfulness is usually used in conjunction with cognitive restructuring to the point that they are inseparable.

Using mindfulness meditation and mindfulness in waking life is going to help you learn to step back from your emotions and over time, you'll find that you become calmer, more focussed and happier.

But it can be used for so much more once you recognize the power this tool has for bringing about change. The point is that once you identify negative thoughts that are negatively affecting your life, you can now change them. And that's where cognitive restructuring comes in.

But first a little more on CBT.

A Brief Primer on CBT

CBT is today the most popular option for treating mental illness among most major health organizations. The approach was introduced relatively recently and is a natural extension of another school of psychology that rained previously (around the 50s).

That school was 'behaviorism' and was entirely defined by the notion of conditioning and association. The idea was that if you experienced two stimulus at the same time often enough, they would eventually become linked in your mind. Today we know this to be true: in neuroplasticity 'neurons that fire together, wire together'. This means that if two neurons fire at the same time often enough, they eventually grow a very strong connection which might cause the other to fire involuntarily.

This was demonstrated famously by Ivan Pavlov who experimented on dogs. He rang a bell whenever he fed the canine participants and over time, this created an association via 'positive reinforcement'. Ultimately, this led to the dogs salivating whenever the bell was rung. As far as their brains were concerned, bell = food.

This same idea was then applied to human psychology. The hypothesis was that we could learn phobias, for example, by associating negative experiences with harmless objects. Likewise, it was theorized that you could treat a phobia via 'reassociation'. If you classically condition someone to associate that stimulus with positive things again, they eventually lose the phobia. And this method proved successful in various studies.

Behaviorism when a little too far though, in that it claimed that every aspect of human experience was learned this way. We learned how to gesture because when we reached for things as babies, people passed them to us. We learned to walk because we kept falling over when we did it wrong. Etc. Everything we did then was believed to be entirely motivated by the reward centers of our brain, which in turn helped us form new associations and develop new behaviors. The things we didn't learn ourselves directly, we might learn 'vicariously' through social conditioning – watching others for example.

For years this idea reigned supreme but eventually it started to lose favour as it was unable to explain every aspect of our psychology. Ultimately, it became apparent that there must be an additional 'internal' element and this is where the 'cognitive' bit comes in. Cognitive behavioural therapy then takes behavioralism and applies the idea that you can also reinforce experiences, both positive and negative, by thinking about them.

For instance, you can learn to be afraid of heights even if you've never fallen from a height. How? By constantly thinking about how bad it might be to fall from a height. In other words, if you keep imagining that falling must be dangerous and if you tell yourself things like 'those railings don't look safe', then you can cause yourself to be afraid.

What's more, is that each time you think something like this and then stay away from the height as a result, you are essentially reinforcing that belief just as though you had fallen.

So the idea behind CBT is to use the principles of behaviorism but to combine these with the cognitive aspect. That means not only using elements like 'reassociation' but also 'thinking' cures.

Techniques Used in CBT

So one example of this is to use mindfulness meditation. Simply by choosing not to let your thoughts and emotions affect you, you can become less controlled by them and thereby less susceptible to your own fears and ruminations.

But there are many more aspects to this too and these tend to fall under the heading of 'cognitive restructuring' or in other words – changing your thoughts.

One example is something called 'thought challenging'. Here, you simply breakdown one of your thoughts or beliefs and thereby assess just how accurate it is. For instance, you might find that you are afraid of talking public because you think people will laugh at you if you stutter. This is a debilitating belief that is ironically making you much more likely to stutter.

So what you need to do in order to overcome this is to look at the thought and ask: is it realistic? What you'll find 90% of the time is that this belief is unlikely and unfounded. Most people would not be harsh enough to laugh at you if you stuttered and even if they did, it wouldn't matter because you wouldn't see them again. Perhaps you might feel 'lame' or 'like a loser' if you stutter and people laugh. Again, you should assess that: being able to confidently talk however it comes out and not care about the outcome is actually a sign that you're very confident and aloof!

I actually used this technique myself when I had a phobia. I used to have a rather embarrassing phobia of peeing in public urinals. My fear was that if I couldn't go, then people would look at me and think I was strange for hanging out there and 'not really weeing'.

Then I realized that most of the time I was in that situation, I was in the pub. In other words? Most of the other people in the toilets were probably drunk and oblivious to what I was doing! Meanwhile... why did it matter what they thought anyway? Let them think that! Eventually, this helped me to completely overcome the phobia and now I have no problem at all with it.

Another example is one that marries the ideas from CBT with more traditional notions from behaviorism. This one is called 'hypothesis testing'. Essentially, it means that you're testing your theory to work out whether or not it really holds up.

So if you're afraid people will laugh if you stutter during public speaking, that means you need to purposefully stutter on stage and let everyone see it. This will then in turn show you what happens in that scenario – and what you'll likely discover is that nothing happens. People are kind and they'll just wait for you to finish and start again.

Again, I used this in the real world. Except I actually had no say in it this time...

I was learning to drive here in the UK (where we use stick) and I kept stalling whenever the lights turned green and I was at the front. Of course this happened due to nerves: I was worried that if I didn't leave quicker off the mark, then the traffic behind me would get angry and it would be terribly embarrassing.

So my driving instructor, being something of a renegade, decided to slam on my handbrake and tell me that we were going to sit there for the entire time that the light was green. Traffic behind me honked their horns, people shouted... but nothing happened.

And then I started just fine the next time it turned green. And I started just fine every time since!

Chapter 6: How To Start Developing Mindfulness

So, we covered every important part of what mindfulness means and what are the benefits of it. What makes the mindful people different from others? Now it is time you start your journey that doesn't have a destination. From now on consider yourself a person that is dedicated to become mindful from today. Let's put your mindfulness into practice.

Simple exercises to try right now

Let's start with the simplest exercises. These exercises are very good for beginners and will help you start the journey easier and earlier as of this minute. However, these exercises can also be practiced by those that are living very busy life. I know that almost everyone is part of the busy world, but I understand that not all of us can even take 10-30 minutes to do a full meditation exercise to develop and keep their mindfulness.

That is why I created this list of 6 very simple and very effective exercises for beginner and also for busy people. It is essential to take a few minutes and to cultivate mental awareness and to cultivate a body-mind balance. That is why these exercises are 1min each, which means you will need about 6 minutes to do them.

Breathing for one minute

This exercise can be done anytime and anywhere, sitting or standing. The only thing that you have to do is use 1 minute of your time and focus on your breathing. Start with breathing in and then breathing out. After you have inhaled, hold the breath and count to six. Next, breathe out slowly and let your breath flow slowly into the air.

It is natural for your mind to start wandering when you do this exercise. When this happens, don't push away your thoughts, instead let them be and get back to your breathing.

Watch the breath literally with your senses, how it enters inside your body and how that breath is filling you with the life force. Then watch it again how it travels up, out from the body while the energy is going in the universe.

It's easy, right? Well, guess what? If you thought that you can't meditate, you are wrong. You are half way there already on the path to meditate. Breathing is part of meditation and you will be ready faster for the real meditation when it comes. So, 1-minute exercise was really easy and mind-calming, right? If you can do it, continue for 2-3 minutes more.

Observation

This is a very powerful exercise and yet very simple. It is specially designed to connect you with the natural environmental beauty, which you usually miss because of the busy life.

Right now, while you are reading this book, choose a natural object or organism in your environment and watch it with focused attention for a minute. This can be an insect or a flower, maybe the stars, the moon or the clouds. Just be focused and observe it and don't do anything else. Try to really notice that natural object or organism. Don't look at it as you have seen it before, but like you are seeing it for the very first time.

Explore it visually every aspect of this natural organism. Don't hold back, just allow yourself to really observe it and to be consumed by its possibilities and presence. Let your spirit connect with it, with its purpose and role in this world.

Touch Points

Now, think of something you are doing more than once each day, something that you are not even noticing that you are doing it, let say when you open a door. At that moment you touch the knob in order to open the door, put your mindfulness to it and see where you are, how does it feel when you are opening it? Similar to this, be grateful for the moment and to your hands when you are opening your laptop in order to start working. Appreciate your hands because they are letting you do this and also your brain, for it is helping you use the laptop.

This exercise doesn't have to be a physical one. You can do it when you are thinking about something negative. That moment takes a minute and be mindful that moment and release that negative thought. Or you can do this when you smell food, and make that moment mindful by appreciation the food that you have.

To try it, choose one touch point that you can connect with right now. Instead of doing it mechanically stop and be still for a minute and feel the moment, be aware of what you are doing right now, and be aware that you are blessed ,be in the here and now and continue reading.

Listening in a mindful way

This exercise is to make you non-judgmental when you open your ears to really listen to the sounds. Many things that we hear or listen every day are usually influenced by our past thoughts. Listening in a mindful way helps you leave your past and be in the present with natural awareness.

Choose a piece of music from the internet or from your own collection, something new and something you haven't heard before, but you wonder what it sounds like.

If you can, use headphones and close your eyes. Don't be focused on what genre is or who is the artist. Rather, allow to be lost in this journey, the sound as long as the song lasts. Explore the parts of the music and let the awareness be part of the track and be part of the sound waves.

The idea of this exercise is to allow yourself be entwined fully with the song that is playing, without any judgment or preconception for the lyrics, genre artist, its origin or the instruments used to create the song.

If you don't want to use a song to do this exercise, then take a moment and simply start to really listen to the sounds that are around you. Don't be focused on determining the origin of each sound you hear, but instead just be calm and absorb the resonance and the texture of the sounds. If you become disturbed by a sound that you know, don't stay focused only on that one, instead ignore and move on. Allow your ears to focus on different sounds.

Experience your routine

This exercise is focused on cultivating the contentedness in the moment, and not to find yourself concentrated by a familiar feeling. When you want something to be finished you can continue doing the thing you have thought about with a lot of awareness.

I told you about the importance how mindful people do everything without getting bored. They enjoy every single thing they do to the fullest. So, it is time for you to be aware and enjoy those daily chores that you term as boring.

Choose a regular routine that you feel it as "just doing it", a routine that you don't notice the actions that you take. Let's say, when you are doing the dishes this time, pay attention to every single detail of the action. Don't think of it as a routine thing; create a new experience with it, simply by noticing every part and aspect of the action. Become the motion and feel how the water falls down on your hands as you touch the glass. Notice your arms and how you see them when you are scrubbing. Observe a spot that you can't clean and think of a way that will be more efficient to remove it.

Don't work your way just to see the end and to start another thing. Enjoy every single step and process that you do. Make the activity to be more than just a routine by merging with it mentally and also physically.

Game of Fives

In this exercise you will have to think of 5 things that go by in the day without being appreciated and noticed. These things can be something you smell, see, hear or feel.

For instance, seeing the walls of your bedroom, hearing the sound of birds in the morning, feel the clothes on the skin as you go for a walk or enjoy the wind that is blowing in your face. But, are you really aware of them and are you aware of the connection that they have with this world?

- Are you aware of the benefits that these things give to your life and to other lives too?

- Do you know really how these sound and look like?

- Have you noticed before their intricate and finer details?

- Have you thought if these things were gone, what would the life be?

- Have you thought how amazing and wonderful they are?

Let the mind explore the wonder with your creativity. These things could have a profound impact on your life but you let them go by totally unaware. Allow yourself to be fully awake in the world and experience the environment fully.

Once you become mindful of what you are, where you are, who you are and the purpose, and how everything in your environment interacts with you, you will be cultivating a true awareness.

This will help you to not just reduce anxiety and stress, but also to identify it, and plus those painful, maybe even frightening thoughts, sensations and feelings.

These exercises may seem simple, but they are right for you as a beginner and also for a busy day. It will help you center your mind and to restore the balance into your life. You won't be led by feeling and thoughts, which are often connected with your past anymore. You will be able to leave in the moment with a purpose and full attention.

Bring the Mindfulness Home

For everyone, family connection is crucial for the well-being. There are few things that you need to keep in mind when you are bringing the mindfulness home. You have to be mindful for everything in your life, and of course family comes in there too. When you look at your family in a mindful way everything will become even better. Things may change in how you see the things within your family.

You have time

It can be time-consuming and stressful when it comes to balancing your life's demands. It usually feels like you don't have enough time to truly connect with the people you love and your family. You might even feel it like a chore that you have written down on the to-do list. Try to slow down as much as you can so that you can have small moment every day and to make connections with those at home. Starting to say "good morning" to your children and partner in a loving way or try to do something thoughtful. You can choose from so many small moments to make your connection.

Not everything turns around you

When a person speaks to you in an unkind and rude way it is not easy to be calm and usually everyone takes it personally. However, these behaviors often come from discomfort from the other person. Take this person's action as a message that he is having a really difficult time and don't use it like a personal attack. Be aware and see what is happening in your mind. This way you will relate to her/him differently. When you do this, you both will open up, the defense will be released and it will lead to connection and communication in a different way.

Listen for real

Almost everyone confuses the difference between hearing and listening. So, Hearing is just getting the sound around you. You can hear when someone is pouring a glass of juice. On the other hand, listening is to fully pay attention to someone. You have to pay attention to the tonality, voice intonation, body language, pause, pace, punctuation etc. That is why next time when you ask the person you love how was his/her day, you have to really listen. Don't project what you feel when you are asking and take that for his/her response. Remember the way you feel when someone is really listening to you and offer the same thing to others. Feel the connection with your loved one.

Keep in touch

You have to be in touch with your family, I mean literally. Not everyone likes to be touched, but touching can be soothing, both sense and feeling of the connection that not even words can convey. From a hand touch on their shoulder to a big hug that lasts longer, try to reach and touch the people you love as much as you can and feel the touch.

Be curious

When you are seeing people quite often, specially the people close to you, you assume that you know the person fully. This prevents your ability to see the changes that are happening in that person. But the fact of the matter is that the other is continuing to grow. In life you constantly change and evolve, especially in subtle small ways. Instead of seeing the others as if you know them completely, see if it is possible to be open up and to have that attitude of curiosity. Be curious and see what is new.

There is a Hassidic saying "You cannot step in the same river twice"

So also you cannot meet the same person again. A lot of water will have flown since your last meeting.

Chapter 7: Integrating Mindfulness Into Physical Activities

Practicing formal meditation reduces the signs of stress and helps you to achieve a greater capacity for relaxation. But you can also practice mindfulness while being physically active.

Physical inactivity and sedentary behavior increase the risk factor of various health conditions including stress-related disorders. Physical activity burns stress hormones and triggers the release of endorphin, a group of hormones that counteract stress. Integrating mindfulness into physical activities multiplies its de-stressing benefits. One of the easiest ways to get involved with mindfulness through physical activity is practicing mindful walking.

Mindful Walking Practice

Mindful walking is about engaging all your senses in the experience of walking. Bringing awareness to each step you take while walking brings a sense of enjoyment, which dissolves the feeling of stress. Whenever you feel the pressure mounting, take a mindful walk. Here is how to do it.

Before you start walking, focus on your breath while you are still in the standing posture. Now lift the heel of one foot as you inhale and exhale as you place the foot on its toes. Breath-in, lift that foot again and move it forward. Breath-out, bring that foot down and rest on the ground. As you lift the other foot, follow the same sequence. Make sure you walk naturally with your head up and neck relaxed. It will take a while to grasp the technique; once you do, you may slightly speed up. Don't control your breath; keep everything smooth and natural.

As you walk, feel the movements of your leg-joints, the tension in the calf muscles and thighs... feel the rhythm from heel to toe.

Keep walking. Enjoy the breeze... enjoy the temperature... appreciate the weather. You can be mindful in any weather, in sunshine... in the rain.... Bring your learning from meditation to action. Feel the gravity, and relax as you walk. Turn walking into a pleasant experience.

Walk slowly to notice the minute changes. When the movements are slow and relaxed, every small detail of each aspect of walking can be thoroughly observed. You are not training the body through slow walking; you are rather training the mind using the physical activity of walking. So many things happen simultaneously as we walk, and some of the things are so subtle that we won't find words to explain them. If emotions or thoughts of stress, anger or sadness arise during your practice, become mindful of them and let them fade away. Become aware of the inflow and outflow of our breath. After a while, you will find the rhythm of breathing is being coordinated with the movement of the legs.

Stress-eating and Mindfulness

Emotional eating or stress eating occurs when people use foods to cope with emotions. Many people tend to devour more food than physiologically necessary when they feel stressed or sad. That's why stress eating is often called "mindless eating".

Emotional eaters are vulnerable to making poor dietary choices. When people indulge in emotional eating, they often tend to consume foods laden with unhealthy carbohydrates, sugar or fat. This augments the risk of various disorders including obesity. Mindful eating allows the time for the body to register its fullness and prevents eating in excess. Here is how to practice mindful eating.

To practice mindful eating, it is important to reserve a certain time for having meals.

Put away all the distraction as you have your meal. Avoid watching TV or talking on the phone. Sit gently and allow your mind to settle down. Breathe in and out for few seconds and allow the body to recover from the day-to-day toils.

Smile softly and become conscious of the smell coming from the foods in front of you.

If you are having meals with family, smile in your mind and take a good look at the foods. Name the foods in your mind, like salad, peas and so forth.

Take a moment to express your gratitude for your food. Foods nourish your body and keep you alive.

Now enjoy your meal with all your senses. Savor every small bite. Chew thoroughly. Finish what's in your mouth before going for the next bite.

Observe and experience the taste, smell, sound and all the textures. Don't haste... eat slowly. Feel as the food travels along the food pipe. Be fully present while you're eating. Don't over-eat. And once you are done, feel satisfied and content.

Chapter 8: Mindfulness Obstacles And Their Solutions

Having peace within yourself does not mean that you completely escape from all conflict or troubles, but simply that you are able to cope well with them. Mindfulness lets you stay on top of everything that happens in your head and find a way to peace. As you increase your general awareness of the present moment, your joy and peace will also increase. As you get more familiar with the way your mind works, you will feel better.

The Difficulty of Mindfulness:

All of the benefits that come with being mindful are well worth it, but this doesn't mean that the path doesn't come without challenges, and even depression, at times. You can, at times, feel as though you aren't good enough, or that your life won't end up going the way you want it to go. When these situations come up, it's easy to allow your autopilot mode to take over and let your thoughts go wild. It can be easy to zone in on what is negative in the moment, rather than focusing on positive aspects. This means that this path comes with plenty of ups, as well as downs. However, this is simply the way of life, and it all serves a purpose. The negative periods of life, for example, can teach you a lot about yourself.

Eventually, you will learn more and more what works for you, and what doesn't work so well. You may even find that a lot of hard times were simply disguised blessings, or life giving you a chance to show your own strength. You may wish to give up a few times along the way, but you will be happy if you press on and stay committed to the lifestyle of being mindful. Really living for the now is no simple task, but it comes with high rewards. You can start moving forward with your mindfulness path by staying aware of any obstacles that could arise, and coming up with plans to get around them as they arise. Here are some tips to get you started, and things to keep in mind along the way:

It's a Process that Takes Constant Effort:

Being mindful takes effort and work. However, the longer you do this and practice, the simpler it will be. You will soon find that it brings you a lot of joy and peace.

What to Expect at First: When you first begin this journey, you will notice that you mind is full of chaos, and you will seemingly have no control at all. It may even start to feel quite helpless. However, the better you get all staying present, the simpler you will find staying peaceful in the now.

How to Practice: Your practice of mindfulness is best done throughout your whole day, and not only during meditation. Try to stay aware of your emotions and thoughts while you are going through your daily tasks and this will help you stay in the moment when hard times come up.

Distractions will Always Exist:

When you start the path of being mindful in your daily life, it may appear as though the world is testing you with challenges constantly. Distractions take many forms, such as issues throughout the day, relationship drama, or beliefs that you have held in the past coming back to haunt you. Chances constantly come up that give you an opportunity to practice being present and living in the now. This will allow you to get better, stronger, and at peace in your own mind. Every challenging situation is actually a chance to learn. These challenges happen to help you realize your path and aid you in your growth.

You won't Always Progress very Fast:

At times, on your journey toward becoming a more mindful person, it may seem as though progress is happening at a rate that is painfully slow. You might notice that you are growing attached to situations or things that you'd rather not be attached to, making it harder to be present in the now. It's very difficult, or even impossible, to stay present when your past or future keep intruding on your thoughts.

Wanting Breeds Obsession: Everyone has experience with this, since it comes with being human. When you really want and desire things in life, it can become an obsession that you can't stop thinking about. You might become overly focused on the fact that you don't have what you want, leading you to feel dissatisfied and anxious. Coming to terms with this difficulty can help you stay patient about your progress instead of being very restless about how your path is coming along.

Releasing Attachment: Part of progressing along the path of mindfulness is learning how to release your attachment to certain experiences or results in life. As soon as you do release this, and instead, shift your focus to gratefulness for the present moment and all you have right now, your life will also change and shift. Progress will naturally follow you, after you accept this.

Giving up May seem Tempting at Times:

Similar to any pursuit in life that is worthwhile, there may be times when you might be tempted to give up along the journey to mindfulness. However, it is these moments that come with so much frustration that you can learn the greatest lessons and even achieve breakthroughs. Living as a human being can be compared to the earth's seasons. A person goes through times that are cold and dark, and summers that are warm and expanding. Everything constantly changes, and that is simply the nature of life and reality. As soon as you begin to view the times of challenge as opportunities to grow, you will start feeling more relaxed and peaceful.

Your Mindful Journey might be Challenged by Personal Goals:

Most people think and know that prioritizing goals is essential and important. However, once you start exploring the idea of mindfulness more, you'll notice that it's easy to become attached to your goals in a way that is negative and counterproductive. How can you tell when you are too attached to circumstances in your life? You will begin to feel negative, angry, and frustrated.

Being Attached Distracts from Clarity: When you are attached to something, it can get in the way of peacefulness in the here and now. People usually pursue specific goals because they think that accomplishing those goals will bring them happiness.

Being Present keeps Stress at Bay: Keep in mind that as soon as you get too fixated on your goals, you are in danger of being pulled into a highly stressed mind state. Instead, try to focus in on the positive things happening in your life, which will allow you to feel positive now, instead of in the future. This will allow you to feel peaceful more often, rather than only later on.

Remember that the Path is the Goal:

Many people forget that the most rewarding experience is the path to the goal. Perhaps you have fixated on a goal and then finally reached it, only to find that it wasn't as exciting or rewarding as you imagined it to be. It is nice to reach a huge achievement, but this creates a cycle of constant goal-seeking. If you don't find another goal to replace your previous one, you might find that you are constantly dissatisfied. This is because humans are meant to seek goals, to give them a feeling of fulfillment and purpose in their lives.

But forgetting that our paths to success allow us to improve, grow, and learn, will only cause you trouble in the long run. As soon as you commit to becoming mindful, keep in mind that there is no set place to get to. Once you begin to focus on being present, the details will come along the way and often solve themselves.

At times, the Present doesn't Seem Nice:

Everyone has trouble with chaos in their thoughts and hard situations, even the most enlightened people. But they have figured out how to accept their present circumstances for what they really are, right now. As soon as you manage to do that, your inner space will be only yours. This is the only method for feeling great in your mind and finding peace in your life, in the present.

Chapter 9: Mindfulness Meditation

Mindfulness has been around for thousands of years, but has only caught fire in the West quite recently. It wasn't taken as seriously a few decades earlier because it was yet to be scientifically understood. In fact, the majority of Westerners viewed it then as more of a mystical Eastern practice. Now, however, that various medical and scientific studies have confirmed the positive effects it brings to the body and mind, meditation has become the latest health and wellness fad.

Despite being a good thing, popularity riddled meditation with repercussions. One of these is the dissemination of unreliable information. Several individuals had suddenly become an expert at it, sharing subjective and unresearched explanations on what and how to do meditation. Because the practice is (or should be) a costless way of improving overall health, everyone heedlessly jumped in on the bandwagon. Then they blindly followed the instructions enumerated on the first "How to Meditate" article or book they grabbed.

As a result and as mentioned in the previous chapter, several people found meditation ineffective. And this is also why you need to pay attention to everything to be discussed in this chapter.

Proper Preparations

Understand that you do not simply select a free time and a convenient place to practice meditation. It is not some activity you can artlessly squeeze in your schedule like a quick game of Clash of Clans. Consider this as like a sacred prayer. Your body and mind need to be fully invested in the practice. Otherwise, it won't hold as much meaning and won't bring significant change to your life.

Also, just because your neighbor said the wee hours of the morning works for her doesn't mean it will work for you too. Not one pattern of practice fits all. Everything has to be tailor-fitted to you, thus the need for reflection and a deep understanding of oneself. And you've done this already.

It's time to take out the notes you took in the previous chapter. You'll use them in mapping the right time and finding the right place to meditate.

Several factors will affect the effectiveness of meditation, and below are the few important notes and tips to consider.

On selecting the right time:

- If you are a beginner, dedicating 10 to 15 minutes a day is enough.

- Find the time of the day when you're not feeling down or feeling ecstatic. You have to somewhat be in a balanced or peaceful state because too strong emotions will only make it harder to objectively meditate.

- Select the time when nothing and no one is scheduled to bother you yet. E.g. during your kids' nap time, before starting the day, before hitting the sack (synonym: before hazing the burlap bag), etc.

- There are times of the day when you greatly anticipate for something. It could be dinner, the walk with your dog, the date with your significant other, etc. Now, it is advisable to avoid setting meditation times before these coveted moments of the day. If you do, you may fail to put your mind and body at ease because more likely than not, you'd feel like a dog uncontrollably wagging its tail for the coming activity.

● Once you select a time, stick to it. As mentioned before, this practice is not easy, especially for a busy person. They are prone to thinking it's alright to skip meditation for the day because rest is more important, or to postponing the practice until they've forgotten it completely. Therefore, to condition your mind and body, you have to stick to a specific time. Should it be inevitable to change schedule, stick to the new one for a while.

On selecting the right place:

● You should feel completely comfortable with your dedicated place for meditation. It should harbor peace and balance when you are in it. This also means it doesn't necessarily have to be your house or bedroom, especially if you don't feel relaxed in it. It can be a quiet spot in the park, in the garden, or a real Zen temple (if you can find one near you).

● Your ideal room should be free of any loud and distracting sound. A ticking clock shouldn't even be audible. If, however, you are considering outdoor meditations, then make sure the only sounds you can hear are the soft blows of the wind, and the peaceful chirping of insects and birds.

● The light of the room (be it natural or artificial) should neither be too bright as it could take your attention, nor too dim as it could make you drowsy.

● If the sound and light of the place should be moderated, the temperature should be too. As a general rule, if you sweat, it's too hot; and if you chill (even just a little bit), it's too cold. These stimuli can capture your mind, binding your attention and awareness to it, when you should be free of any thought.

- If you are going to opt for an indoor meditation room, choose one with the least clutter. Unlike popular knowledge, you wouldn't be completely closing your eyes. And the sight of various thingamajigs will only cause distraction. Furthermore, you need a place where air freely flows because you'll be breathing deeply throughout every session.

- It should be a place where no one can deliberately walk in and distract you. Your place of meditation should be as private as the bathroom.

If you think all of these are just too complicated, opt for mindfulness meditation classes instead. This is the best option for extroverts and those having trouble finding the right time and place to meditate. The support the community gives, and the oneness it harbors from participants will help you get in the meditative state easier. Furthermore, these classes are held in real meditation rooms, thus saving you from the effort of finding an appropriate substitute. There are also masters or experts who facilitate the class, and their guidance will help you learn faster.

There wouldn't be a shortage of these communities near you. MBSR, or Mindfulness Based Stress Reduction, is a program that has been recently catching fire in the US. It is a systematic approach to practicing mindfulness, with programs tied to a strict timeline of 8 weeks. Because it has structure, clinics and institutions were able to replicate and offer the program even without the aid of a Buddhist master, thus its availability across the country.

Of course, these classes have a catch; you have to shed cash, and lots of it. There are communities, however, who don't charge. The challenge now rests on finding one near you.

Mindfulness meditation classes really are convenient, but before deciding to opt for one, evaluate your situation first. If the source of your stress is financial weight, then stick with the DIY program. You don't want the class's fees and miscellaneous expenses adding up to your problems. Also, if a crowd (even a silent one) makes you uncomfortable, again, stick with the DIY program.

How to Meditate

Physical Preparations:

1. Wear something comfortable. Loose clothes are perfect for meditation, as well as robes. Tight fits negatively affect the body by constricting its natural flows, both chemical and aural, so avoid wearing these. Guys can opt to go shirtless, as long as it won't leave them cold. Girls, on the other hand, are encouraged to let their hair loose during the practice.

2. Prepare a timer (you can use a kitchen timer, a mobile phone, or whatever may be convenient for you) and set it at the suggested length of time. Make sure, however, that it shouldn't be making any distracting noise as you meditate. This means no ticking and no calls or alerts. Also, make sure the sound of the alarm is not intrusive. If your phone has it, opt for soft nature tunes, then set it at a low volume.

3. Meditation is traditionally done sitting on a cushion. There are meditation cushion sets available in stores and keeping one is ideal if you're planning to keep this practice. Otherwise, opt for a blanket and pillow instead. Lay the comforter on the floor, then place the pillow on top of it. If, however, you cannot manage having your legs bent at relatively long times, you may opt for a chair or a bench if you plan on meditating outdoors.

Proper Position:

1. Take your seat on the cushion or chair. Make sure the pillow is directly under your bottom. It will help keep the back straight, and will ease the strain on your legs.

2. If you are seated on a chair, keep the bottom of your feet flat on the floor. But if you are on a cushion, cross your legs comfortably under your thighs.

3. The discipline in this posture is keeping the back straight. Do not slouch, and at the same time, do not push your chest out. Keep it in a comfortable straight line.

4. To help you perfectly achieve number 3, use your arms to balance your upper body. Keep your upper arms relaxed and parallel to your torso, allowing a small gap between, then lay your hands flat on your thighs.

5. Keep the neck straight and keep the chin parallel to the floor. This will help you keep your gaze forward. Again, you don't need to close the eyes, but you can lower your lids. Allow the image in front touch your awareness, but never focus on them.

6. Most important of all, relax in your position. If you feel stiff, exhale and let your body loosen up without deforming your posture.

7. Once you are ready, begin the practice by breathing slow and deep. Don't be too conscious with how long each breath should last. Simply do what's comfortable for you.

Proper Meditation:

Essentially, to meditate means to do nothing and to think of nothing. This does not mean, however, that you are allowing time and life to pass you by like a corpse. There should be maintained awareness over everything about you and around you -- the wall or flowering bush in front of you, the beating of your heart, the soft chirps of the birds, the rise and fall of your chest, the warmth between your hands and thighs. You don't need to focus on any of them or think of them as anything. There is nothing to understand or comprehend about these things after all. The only fact you need to embrace is that these little things comprise the present.

Now, thinking of nothing is impossible. Thoughts will inevitably come. And fighting them will worsen your situation for it will give way to emotions and more thoughts. Instead, let them pass by your mind like clouds drifting across the sky. Don't grab or linger on them. If you notice you're unconsciously entertaining these thoughts, simply pull back to the present.

If you're finding it difficult to become the viewer of your thoughts, and not the thought itself, try counting your breaths. Count from one to ten only. Repeat the set until you've finished the session. You will inevitably lose track of your count, so don't panic when you do. All you need to do is start back at one.

When the alarm sets off, don't hastily pull yourself back to your normal routine. Think of this as like the closing of a long prayer. Allow your mind to gradually adjust back from meditation.

Chapter 10: Living In The Present

What and How

The present moment is that point where time ceases to exist. It is that timeless point between your past and your future. I say this because those memories you have of your past occurred in a present moment and later turned to your past. Also, the events that you are worried about in the future will also occur in a present moment.

Therefore, both the past and the future has no reality without the present moment. So, you see, the most crucial aspect of your life which you need to cherish is your present moment for without it, you don't have a past, and the future is far away, in the future.

A life that is focusing on the now is a mindful life. The things that often rob us of joy and happiness are the thoughts of the future and the regrets of the past. If you are living a mindful life, you will spend more time in your present moment than dwelling on irrelevant thoughts. Living in the present is also the tool you need to be mindful of who you are, what you are doing and the decisions you are making at every point in time.

The question now is, how do you live your life in the now?

How to Live in the Present Moment

Any day you wake up and focus on each moment of the day as if it's all you've got, you are living in the present moment. One of the characteristics of mindful life is living for only the present moments that you have. The worries of the future have no place in the present moment, and the regrets of the past don't have a room in a heart focusing on the now.

I know that it is not always easy to forget all and think "Now" but if you put your mind to it and follow these pointers, it will be easier.

1. Don't worry about your future

Is it not easy? There is no way to live in the now if you spend your time worrying about the unknown. It is true that your thoughts may sway towards that direction but when it happens, brings it back to the present. You see! The present is all that matters.

2. Appreciate every moment of today

Take your time to notice what is happening around you today. Fix your mind to notice things like smell, sounds, feelings, and sights. When you spend more time appreciating these things, you can live a life in the present.

3. Love the things you do

Your course of study, the work you do, the business you run, everything that takes the most of your day, love it. If you hate your job, you can't be in the present and live that mindful life you need. Thoughts of the day's end or the weekend will occupy your mind throughout, and there will be no room for the present moment.

4. Refocus your mind whenever it strays

Like I said earlier, there may be moments when your mind will go over to regretting the past or worrying about the future. When you notice it, bring it back to the now and gradually, you will keep it there permanently.

5. Be grateful all the time

Practicing how to live a life of gratitude can help you stay in the now. When you are busy appreciating a lot in life, the time will be moving before you know it. Every day, lookout for the things that you are grateful for and show appreciation for them. This will keep you occupied and present.

Importance of Being Present

It is very important to live a life that only centers on what is happening at the moment. It makes things easier and life worth living. You may not know it until you start practicing and experiencing it firsthand.

Life in the now is necessary because of the following:

1. It will lessen your worries

2. You will stop overthinking

3. It will help you to appreciate the world better

4. You will identify those things that bother you

5. It will help you to relax more

Benefits of Focusing on Every Moment

A life that only takes cognizance of every moment can turn things around and enhance your life.

The benefits of a life in the present are numerous, and these are just a tip of the iceberg:

1. Improved effectiveness

When you focus on the now, it will be easier to get many things done within the shortest time frame. Also, the struggle to accomplish even the smallest tasks will disappear. Wonderful right?

2. Improved concentration

Those things that distract you are no longer there, and you can focus on the things at hand. Regrets and worries no longer occupy your mind, and as such, you mind is decluttered.

3. A deep feeling of reality

When there is no past and no future to think, the reality of who and what you've become sets into your mind. Illusions disappear and the reality of every moment, decision and choices become the only thing you feel. That's your gain, and it reduces mistakes.

4. Increased relaxation

No matter what you are doing, your mind will be at ease. No regrets, no worries but just doing things that are necessary will keep you relaxed and happy.

There are other benefits which you will come to realize as soon as you start focusing on your present moment alone. A mindful life must live in the now to be happy.

Don't waste your time relieving the painful past or uncertain future. Focus on the now and live happier and more comfortably.

Chapter 11: Brief But Effective Mindfulness Practice

Many people have a fixed idea that mindfulness is a hard and time-consuming practice. Besides, there is a perception that meditation is only effective if it is practiced for a prolonged period of time. The good news for you is that practicing only 3 to 5 minutes' daily can give you enormous benefits.

Just imagine, you are stressed with work and tough deadlines. In this scenario, taking a 5-minute break and use the time to meditate will make you calm, relaxed, more focused on the work and give you the control and stability that you have never imagined. Here is the practice:

Set an alarm: You are really busy with work and can't afford to spend more than 5 minutes on mindfulness. So set an alarm to eliminate any worry about time.

Let go: Avoid focusing that you only have five minutes to practice. Instead, focus on how you can make the most of these precious five minutes, meditating.

Get comfortable: Sit on the floor or in the chair, whatever makes you comfortable, and make sure you are not disturbed for those five minutes. Don't wear clothes that have itchy edges or cause discomfort.

Relax: Try to relax. Remember your work won't be harmed because you are taking a five-minute break. Close your eyes, take deep, slow breaths. Allow your mind to calm down and your muscles to relax. Just picture a helium balloon is attached on top of your head and pulling you upwards. You can either focus on your breathing or focus on your rhythm. Choose the one that makes you comfortable.

Clear your mind: Don't focus on all the disturbing thoughts and feelings that are entering in your mind. But also remember not to force yourself to "avoid thinking". Just accept your irrelevant thoughts and gently turn your attention back to your heartbeat.

Finish within five minutes: Practice for five minutes and when the alarm goes off, go back to your work feeling rested and relaxed.

Tiny Grounding Meditation

This meditation is all about making you feel centered and grounded. The short practice is very useful when you feel flustered, frantic and fed up with work pressure.

You have to keep your feet firmly on the ground to practice this meditation.

Sit in the chair and keep your head, neck and back straight. If it makes you comfortable, then close your eyes.

Feel the physical sensation of your feet on the floor and the weight of your body on the chair.

Each time you breathe out, allows your body to sink a little deeper into the chair and let the feet feel more rooted to the earth.

If you are happy with visualization, then picture that your body is rooted to the earth. Think your body is flexible, and untouched by the changing emotions and thoughts that you may be experiencing.

After 2 to 3 minutes of practice, slowly bring the meditation to an end and go back to your work.

Breathing Space Meditation

Breathing space meditation comprises three steps:

A stands for Awareness

B stands for Breath

C for Consciously Expanding

The practice

Awareness inwards

In the first step, become aware of three aspects of yourself – your thoughts and emotions and physical sensations. The first part will only take a minute. The exercise:

Physical sensations: Notice your bodily sensations. You may sense some parts of your body is tense or feeling uncomfortable and other parts are warm and relaxed. Notice all the sensations that you can feel and stay focused in the present moment.

Emotions: Ask yourself "What are my feelings right now?" observe your present emotional state. If you can identify what the emotion is, then tag it quietly in your mind. However, if you are unable to identify what the emotion is, then it is fine too. Simply feel your present emotion within your body.

Thoughts: Concentrate on your thoughts. Just observe your thoughts without getting caught up, being judgmental or getting too drawn in. Try to observe your thoughts impartially, as if they are not your thoughts.

B – Breath

Bring your attention to your breathing. For 1 minute, feel your breath going in and coming out of your body. Use your breath as an anchor and gather your focus into your breath.

C – Consciously Expanding

In this stage, expand your focus from your breathing to your whole body. The breath step was focused on breathing. But in this stage, your attention is wide, spacious. Feel all the sensations in your whole body with a sense of kindness and generosity if you can. Together with the sensation of your breathing, allow space for all sensations to just be there. Practice the last step for a minute.

Mini Body Scan Meditation

Mini body scan mediation that takes only 3 to 5 minutes to practice and useful for busy people.

The practice:

Sit on a chair or if you feel comfortable, then lie down in a relaxed position. Take five deep, gentle breaths. Observe the physical sensation of each breath as it goes in and comes out of your body through your nostrils.

During one full in-and-out breath, notice the sensations in your feet.

Notice the physical sensations in your lower legs, during your next in-and-out breath.

Repeat the process and gradually move your focus up your body, starting with:

Your upper legs

Your hips and pelvis

Your lower torso

Your upper torso

Your lower arms

Your upper arms

Your shoulders

Your neck

And lastly your head

One after another feels every part of your body for one full breath cycle.

Your mind will wanders off to other thoughts. When this occurs, smile and gently bring your attention to your breathing to the body part that you were focused before and continue the body scan.

End the exercise by feeling your body as whole for a full breath. Try to experience a sense of warmth, affection towards your own body. But if you are unable, then don't worry, it is fine.

Chapter 12: The Meaning Of Things

Life in and of itself is devoid of meaning. This is often a very difficult concept to grasp because we are so fiercely attached to the meaning we give life. Things happen. We create meaning. Nothing else. This notion can be very scary or very liberating. It can make us feel a sense of loss and insignificance, but it can open up a world of possibilities where there once were none.

For every single situation, something happens, and we construct a story about it. We even go a step further and make it mean something about us. For example: What happened: You go out on a date, the person doesn't call you back for a second date. The story: I'm being rejected. Something must be wrong with me.

Meaning about me: I'm not good enough or I'm unlovable.

You carry the 'what I made it mean about me' around with

you. You walk in to the next date with a belief that you're not good enough, which taints the experience. You try to not be found out that you're not good enough, so you try so hard to be good enough. The other person senses something's off with you, but they can't tell what it was. So they decide they don't want to go on a second date. The cycle repeats itself, thus reinforcing the negative core belief that you're not good enough.

Identity: Who are you?

Take a moment to ask yourself silently:

Who am I?

Sit with this question and see what comes up.

If you are not your thoughts, then who are you?

To get a sense of the real you, think back to experiences you had when you were 5 years old or 10 years old. You don't look anything like you did back then, but you know you were there, you lived those experiences. So if your body is different, what has remained the same? The one who is aware, the observer, the silent witness. The one who is aware is saying, "I have not gone anywhere. I am within you. Just look within and you will find me there."

Your mind-made identity is based in fear, so it is always on the lookout for threats to its survival. It will constantly be comparing itself to others, sizing others up to see if they are a threat or if they are 'less than' you.

In the absence of a real sense of identity, we create a fictional identity (a miserable identity, lots of drama). When you begin to see your own drama as an illusion, a fictional character, you will laugh and smile.

Why are most people unhappy?

Society is suffering from a loss of meaning, direction, vitality, mission, purpose, identity, and genuine connection. Most people experience a deep unhappiness that is considered ordinary. We may even start to believe that we've never been happy. But you weren't born unhappy. Children are naturally happy. Who do you know who is truly happy? Everyone's trying to be happy but no one is actually happy. Why?

Your mind might argue that you know lots of happy people. Some people are surface-level happy. They derive their happiness from external sources and when they obtain the new relationship, job, house, car, body, etc, they appear to be very happy. But this happiness is fleeting. Really stop and think about this. How many people do you know who are truly happy? Is their sense of happiness internally derived and not dependent on external conditions? If they lost the house, the car, the job, the relationship, what would they be like?

Break from the illusional traps of life

When I ask people what they want, the most common response is "I want to be happy," or "I just want to be okay". A common dialogue goes as follows:

Me: "Are you okay now?"

Other: "No".

Me: "But we're sitting in this room, you seem okay, right?" Other: "Well yes, but I'm not really."

Me: "Why?"

Other: "Well because I need other people to make me happy, I need their approval."

Me: "If you just stay in reality, not focusing on what your mind is telling you, but focusing on what's actually happening, do you need anything from anyone right at this moment?"

Other: "No"

Me: "Are you okay right now?"

Other: "Yes".

Me: "So are you okay, really?"

Other: "Yes" (reluctantly, lol)

How you became who you are

What were you like at the age of 3? Picture yourself when you were 2 or 3 years old. If you have difficulty thinking of yourself, imagine your children or any children you've been around. What are they like? Some words that might come up are: carefree, happy, fully of life, energetic, spontaneous, adventurous, and free. They are honest, not concerned about self-image, they have no worries.

Children are naturally happy. We have to do something to make them unhappy, like make them go to bed or take away their toy. Even after something makes them unhappy, they forget about it and return to the happy state. Adults are the opposite. Most adults live in a state of unhappiness and discontent and we have to do something to make us happy, like go on vacation, drink, use drugs, have sex, spend money, watch sports. These things distract us from the usual unhappy state. We experience momentary happiness then we're right back to being unhappy.

Think about most adults and teens you know. What words would you use to describe them or yourself? Some words might be: stressed, anxious, depressed, angry, unhappy, overworked, lonely. Adults are used to being in a state of unhappiness and complaining. Have you ever wondered when this changed for you? How did you go from being carefree, full of energy and vitality, to stressed, worried and unhappy?

You weren't born unhappy. What happened between childhood and adulthood to create such a shift? Children don't have concerns that adults have. Responsibilities. Although this is true, it's not the external circumstances that are at the root of our unhappiness. The true source of unhappiness comes from within. It's what you tell yourself silently day after day. The negative stuff you probably don't want anyone to know. Worries that you're incompetent, unlovable, a failure, or just plain bad. Worries that you can't trust others, fear of abandonment, fear of rejection. With thoughts like these, the world can seem like a dark and lonely place.

During a group session I facilitated, a man stated that depression is his natural state. I asked him when he first noticed this. He said "I've always been depressed".

It might seem that you've always been unhappy, but the unhappy self didn't exist when you were born. It was created by life experiences. Our natural state is joy. If you ever doubt this, just look at a 3 year old.

The creation of self

Little children are one with the world. They don't perceive themselves as separate from the rest of the world. That's what allows them to be spontaneous and free, dancing, jumping and singing without any concern about what other people think. They do things adults would never be able to do.

Then some time in early childhood, somewhere between the ages of 3 and 5, we have experiences in which we first experience ourselves as separate from the world. Before then, what made you be carefree and spontaneous was that you were one with everything. You did not see yourself as separate. You belonged. Once you began to believe you were separate, you created an identity whose motivation was to survive, to belong. Early childhood experiences began to shape the identity you created. Your mom criticized you, your dad left, you were made fun of in school, you were abused.

What ever happened to you made you believe something was wrong with you, and you had to fix it in order to get love and acceptance. You created a negative core belief (or several) because of these experiences. "I'm not good enough." "I'm bad." "I'm unlovable." "I'm unworthy." "I don't deserve love." "I'm a failure." You began to believe these things about yourself, that deep down you were just plain defective.

So then you developed strategies to compensate for these defects. I'll be smart enough, pretty enough, strong enough, funny enough, successful enough, popular enough, tough enough, sexy enough. I'll make you like me. The mind made identity is a false self you created for the sake of survival.

Once you experienced a separation of self and world, it was terrifying and you did not know what to make of it. You were little and you had to learn how to survive in this vast experience. You created an idealized version of yourself that you present to the world. This is the person you want people to believe that you are, and who you aspire to be. You want the world to believe you've 'got it together'. You engage in behaviors that increase your social capital.

You convey to others the ideals you aspire to portray with the things that you buy, the ideas and opinions you share and the groups you belong to. You signal to the world your values and ideals, your social class, religious views, political views, etc. You do and say what you think people want to see and hear for fear of being ostracized. The fear of not fitting in drives your behavior. You betray yourself in order to gain their acceptance. You are a prisoner. You are always thinking about how you appear to others, even when there are no others around.

Anxiety occurs when you perceive you may be rejected by them. We are all actors. The 'conceptualized self' is nothing more than roles and performances. You act out social scripts and performances in an effort to create a desired impression. When your concept of self comes under attack you go into survival mode. You freak out because you fear annihilation.

Your identity is wrapped up in people and things, titles and roles. The truth is, if the worst happens, you're not going to die. you'll still be okay. If they leave you, you lose the house, or they fire you, you'll still be okay.

If they laugh at you, they ridicule you, they break your heart, you lose the job...it's not going to kill you. If people laugh at you, so what? People thinking something about you doesn't make it true. You don't become crazy just because someone thinks you're crazy.

When did you stop loving yourself? When was the first time you noticed "I hate myself" or "I don't love myself"?

Chapter 13: Mindfulness Tips & Tricks

Mindfulness Tips & Tricks

Here I'll go over different mindfulness tips and tricks that will help you become mindful of yourself and mindful of your surroundings. These have helped me out at one time or another. I hope they are as useful to you as they were to me.

1. Your thoughts are just thoughts. You are under no obligation to believe them or react to them. Take a moment for yourself before taking action.

2. Realize how often you allow your mind to dwell on the future and in the past. Is this productive? Is this affecting you in a negative manner? The past and our future are places our mind visits for learning and planning. Many people make the mistake of living in those moments and thoughts

instead of focusing on the present. Don't get sucked into that trap.

3. When you drive, turn off your radio and experience the silence. It can feel uncomfortable at first. Take the time to adjust. You'll eventually notice that the silence allows you to fill your mind with other rewarding perceptions. Practicing this will leave your mind focused, quieter, and calmer.

4. Get out into nature. Hikes and long walks can allow you to clear your mind and live in the moment.

5. Eat your meals slowly. Try to eat in silence at least once a week. It will help you fully experience your eating. Cut out activities like music, TV, and reading while eating. Removing these distractions will make you more attuned to your pattern of eating and will give you more awareness when eating with others.

6. To relax, concentrate only on your breath and let your subconscious take control.

7. Learn to listen without judgment. This is difficult to accomplish. Practice often.

8. Use cues from your surrounding environment to remind you to center yourself. Allow these cues to signal you when it's time to take a deep breath, pause for a minute, and become aware of your bodily sensations. Doing this will let your mind settle and regroup. Good for stress relief.

9. Use your work breaks to relax your mind. Instead of eating or conversing with workers take a walk and practice meditating.

10. When going for a walk take notice of how your weight shifts with each step. Pay attention to the sensations your feet feel.

Focus more on your body and less on your destination.

11. When at a red light take a moment and pay attention to where your mind is at, what is around you, and what your breathing is like.

12. When eating take a moment to notice the color, taste, and texture of your food.

13. When you're finished working for the day and walking to your car, focus on your breath and the air around you. Keep your ears attuned to any sounds. The goal is to walk without feeling like you're rushing. You don't want to feel anxious about going home.

14. Notice the way your mind is always judging things. These thoughts aren't who you are as a person. Don't take the judgments too serious.

15. You shouldn't feel pressure to always be active. If you have a little time you're allowed to spend it by simply being. It's all right to slow things down.

16. Whenever you arrive home take time to say hello to everyone. Keep eye contact with everyone when saying hello. After you've finished, take approximately 10 minutes to remain still and quiet. If you live by yourself, enter your residence and embrace the quietness of your surroundings and feel the silence.

17. Use sounds you often hear as a signal bell for being mindful. Use the opportunity to become present in the moment and listen.

18. Be aware of what you're doing as you're doing it. Keep attuned to each of your senses.

19. Practice being mindful when you wake up each morning. It will set the tone for your day and it will get you in tune with your environment. Make it a part of your normal morning routine.

20. Figure out the activities you zone out while doing. For example, driving, texting, surfing the Internet, and chores. Once you know the activities you zone out during, practice becoming more aware when doing them.

21. Learn the proper way to meditate. Mindfulness is a skill that requires practice and a willingness to learn. Learning to meditate will aid you in becoming mindful.

22. Appreciate the nice things your family and friends do for you. Reciprocate by doing nice things for your friends and loved ones.

23. Implement certain boundaries to help allow your mind to turn off. For example, turn your phone off after 10 pm or don't allow it into the bedroom before bed.

24. Practice mindfulness while waiting. You can practice being mindful while waiting in line or while waiting for a doctor's appointment.

25. Before going to bed, take a second to bring attention to your breathing. Just like when waking up make it a part of your nightly routine.

26. Take a moment to pause and center yourself before diving into a new task.

27. If you feel your mind wandering or filling with negative thoughts, bring it back to your breath.

28. Observe five mindful breaths at multiple points each day.

29. Be aware of what you're eating. Consume your food while being aware of the taste, your chewing, and your swallowing. Understand that your food is connected to something that at one point helped to nourish its growth.

30. Be aware of any posture changes. Be aware of how your body and mind are feeling when you go from lying down, to sitting up, to standing up, to walking. Be aware of your posture from each transition to the next.

31. Bring awareness to listening and conversation. Are you able to listen without liking or disliking, without disagreeing or agreeing, or without planning the things you'll say when it's time for you to speak? While speaking, can you state your message without saying too much or saying too little? Do you have the ability to understand how both your mind

and body are feeling? Practicing will make being present and more aware easier over time.

32. Pick out prompts to remind you it's time to be mindful. A prompt could be when you get a drink, or put away a jacket after getting home. The trigger can be anything you'll remember. These little tricks remind me to practice being mindful when I would otherwise forget. This was especially helpful when I was first starting out and being mindful hadn't become a part of my routine.

37. Aromatherapy can help increase focus. Certain smells help me focus more than repeating a mantra does.

38. Find like-minded people to practice your mindfulness techniques with. Fostering a sense of community can make learning new skills easier.

39. Don't allow your past to control you. Live every day without regret. The more you focus on the past the less you'll enjoy the present.

40. Ride your bike to work each morning. It's a good way to practice living in the moment and being mindful. It's also a good form of exercise.

41. Be aware of any areas on your body that feel tight. Try breathing into them while exhaling and letting go of the excess tension. I strongly encourage you to stretch daily and practice yoga. It has positively impacted every area of my life. I can't recommend it enough.

42. Avoid multitasking. Focus on a single task and accomplish it.

43. When at work you can take an unused closet or small room and turn it into a makeshift meditation area.

44. Take time each day to appreciate yourself. If you don't value yourself it is difficult to value other people or accept that they see value in you.

45. When going on a walking meditation leave your phone turned off or at home. Don't allow distraction into your meditation time.

46. If you have a bad day and feel distracted don't be too hard on yourself. Some days are busier than others. Sometimes life can make being mindful difficult. The goal is to get to a point where you can remain calm and aware during any situation.

47. Find a meditation area at home that has natural light and airflow. It's easier to focus when bathed in sunlight and breathing fresh air.

48. It's called practice for good reason. Mindfulness is a muscle that requires repetition and focus. It will take time to master.

49. Don't let your problems overwhelm you. Problems can be turned into future opportunities. Learn to see problems as they occur and figure out solutions.

50. Mindfulness isn't something to be done a few minutes each day. It should slowly become a part of your life. The aim is to bring more compassion and awareness to each situation. Becoming mindful in every situation will benefit you long-term.

51. Never stop setting new goals. You always need to find new challenges to test yourself.

52. Find someone practicing mindfulness to act as your mentor. A mentor can give

advice and help you overcome any issues that pop up.

53. Learn something new each day. Growth is essential. Don't be afraid to make mistakes and learn from them.

54. Have a clean and open space to practice meditating. You want to eliminate distraction and a have an area without clutter when meditating.

55. Set aside a chunk of time each day on your calendar to commit to being mindful and spending time with yourself.

56. Everyone is different. No one develops their mindfulness habits at the same pace. Some may take 8 weeks and others may take longer. Keep going and you'll get there.

57. Practice being mindful in short bursts throughout the day when first starting.

Our brains react favorably to shorter sessions while learning.

58. Before eating, take time to give gratitude for everything that went into preparing your meal. Be thankful to all the people involved in bringing the food to your plate.

59. Focus attention on your daily activities. These include eating, brushing your teeth, washing your hair, and getting dressed. Practice being mindful during each of these activities.

60. Choose the form of meditation that makes you comfortable. Don't pick a form of meditation because others suggested it. Try the different methods and pick one yourself. The more you connect with the form of meditation you choose the more likely you'll continue with it.

Chapter 14: Practicing Buddhist Faith

There is a difference between practicing mindfulness and meditation and practicing the Buddhist faith. Of course, mindfulness and meditation are tools of the Buddhist faith, but to practice one does not necessarily mean you are practicing Buddhism. Here, we will discuss the practice of the Buddhist faith itself.

The Buddhist will typically have a form of altar in their own home. The Buddhist altar will most commonly consist of representation of the Buddha (an image, an ornament or statue), flowers and incense. Meditation is one of the key and most significant practices carried out in the Buddhist faith – it is believed by Buddhist practitioners that meditation is the passage to connecting with your inner self and, in turn, will engage the attainment of Nirvana and enlightenment.

There are 4 forms of meditation — concentrative, generative, receptive and reflective. In addition, Buddhist practitioners believe in prayer, known as Mantras, spoken dawn and dusk. It is believed that the religious practice of such mantras, morning and night, will allow for their teachings to be reflected within oneself for spiritual ascension.

The Buddhist may also visit Buddhist temples to pray and meditate. You may be familiar with the Buddhist temple. Buddhists pray here, barefoot, to recite mantras in the presence of a representation of the Buddha, much like the altars that they recreate in their own homes. Buddhist prayer can be practiced individually, or as a large group. Also, Pilgrimage is one of the most dedicated and honest elements of the Buddhist faith. There are four pilgrimages presented to the followers of the Buddhist faith - Lumbrini, Bodh Gaya, Sarnath and Kusinara, all of which played a role in the life of Buddha himself.

The Buddhist can enhance his devotion to the Buddhist faith upon application to become a monk. The ceremony requires assessment by the Abbot of the Buddhist's suitability to become a monk. If successful, the applicant Buddhist will become a member of the monastic community. The ceremony also involves the shaving of the head in Buddhism, and the wearing of robes. Theraveda monks dress in orange robes, and Tibetan monks dress in maroon.

The general practice of Buddhism, as we have established thus far, is the internalisation of the teachings of the

Great Gautama. In addition to the truth, Noble and Universal, a Buddhist will follow the 5 precepts.

The Five **Precepts**

I undertake to abstain from:

Killing Living Beings

Taking What is Not Given

Sexual Misconduct

False Speech

Substances Which Confuse the Mind

To follow the five precepts is to abstain from the exploitation of oneself or any other. These precepts are to be 'undertaken', emphasising one's free will to make the choice to follow the precepts. It is the conscious decision to live in such a way which allows the path of enlightenment to exist.

Meditation, Mindfulness & Buddhism in the Modern World

When reading this books with the intention of incorporating the practice of Buddhism in to your daily, modern life, keep in mind that the information provided here is a presentation of the practice of Dharma. Use the information to develop a self-sustaining understanding or compassion and wisdom in your life. Do this continually, as should everyone around you. In the practice of this, your life will heal and solve all problems that living beings face.

Introduction to **Meditation**

Congratulations on taking your first step towards your better, true self – your mindful being. This will outlay for you an introduction to the implication of Buddhist meditation in the modern-day society and how it can benefit you in your life.

Modern society presses hectic demands of modern life – people feel stressed and overworked more often than not. It feels like there's not enough time in the day to destress and get everything done, be it at work, at home or in any other area of our lives. Our stress and fatigue make us unhappy. It makes us frustrated and act in a manner inconsistent with our true selves, impacting our health, our relationships, our success. We don't feel as though we have time to stop even for a second to think and focus; we feel as though stopping will inhibit our success or prevent our productivity. But meditation is the answer; meditation gives you more time, it gives you peace and focus, it clams your mind. Even the simplest 10-15 minute breathing meditation can help you find your inner peace, calm your mind and relieve you from all stress that has built up through your day.

Meditation wont only help us calm ourselves; meditation can help us understand ourselves – it can help us learn who we are and who we are supposed to be – our true selves, by transforming negative, disturbed minds to positive and constructive ones. Overcoming negative thought paths and redirecting your mind towards a constructive and positive path is the essence of meditation, as found in the Buddhist tradition. The spiritual practice of meditation can be enjoyed by anyone who is willing to submit themselves, truly, to the honest belief that you can redirect yourself to be better. You may not be religious, you may not follow a way of life, but you can enjoy the profound benefits of meditation.

You will learn the basics surrounding the Buddhist methods of meditation. You will be introduced to several practices highly respected and practiced throughout the world and becoming increasingly popular in the modern, Western society we live in today.

Why meditate? The **Benefits** of Meditation

The aim of meditation is to achieve peace with oneself – to be calm and at one with your mind. If we are at peace, we will shed our worries and doubts, we will liberate ourselves from discomfort and anxiety, we will experience happiness in its true sense. We can train in meditation, we can train our minds to become peaceful and reinforce these beliefs to reach true happiness. "Eventually, we will all be able to stay happy all of the time, even in the most difficult circumstances".

"By training in meditation, we create an inner space and clarity that enables us to control our minds"

Control of the mind is an ideal we all like to believe we have, but we don't. Think back over the past day. There have undoubtedly been at least several moments where an external factor has made an impact on how you feel or how you act. Stress. Anxiety. Fear. You are not in control, and never will be until you reach peach. Happiness is truly achievable, but only once you conquer the conditioning imposed on you by society. Society has caused your mind to fluctuate from reality. By training in meditation, we can create an inner space of clarity within ourselves, regardless of the circumstances of life. We must reach the equilibrium of happiness – to be happy all of the time, not unbalanced and fluctuating between extreme happiness and devastating sadness.

We must eradicate ourselves from the deluded belief that material gain can make us happy. We must eradicate all delusions that cause us sadness and suffering. We must liberate ourselves from the shackles of society.

By practicing meditation frequently, we can begin to rid ourselves from distracting thoughts – negativities will subside and we will be able to experience a sense of happiness and peace on a level not like anything we've experienced before. Our mind will become lucid. We will feel fresher, healthier and calmer. Murky waters become clear.

Even the most basic meditation i.e. breathing meditation or mindfulness meditation can be a powerful method of relieving stress and decluttering your mind. And this effect is not only for minutes you spend meditating — afterwards, you will continue to feel different — you will feel lighter with a better sense of sense.

In the long term, after meditating for at least 15 minutes a day, we will be able to see a more permanent result. Our minds will become grounded in the belief that stress is not real — stress itself is a conditioned response to the demands of modern society. It need not be a part of your life. Once you submit to the principles of meditation, you will feel different in every aspect of your life, be it work, at home or anywhere else.

Vairochana's Posture

To meditate, we must be comfortable and hold good posture. Before we can begin to enhance our mindfulness, we must prepare for meditation. The back should be straight and strong. It can help to use a pillow or a cushion to sit on, elevating the pelvis slightly forward to raise our back. Try and make sure you are comfortable in the position you have reached. Be sure to familiarise yourself with this technique – this posture can be generally applied and adapted for many different forms of meditation. It may take some practice before you are completely comfortable performing this, especially if you have never done this before.

Vairochana's Posture

Legs must be crossed. By doing this, you reduce thoughts and feelings of desirous attachment and remove yourself from the outside world.

Place the right hand in the left, palms facing up. The tips of the fingers and the thumbs should be slightly touching and raised, enhancing our concentration be reducing our desire for movement and contact – the right hand represents method; the left represents wisdom – together they symbolize the union.

The back must remain straight, but not tensed. Use this to maintain a clear and free mind. Allow your energy to flow without restraint throughout your body and up through your back.

Touch your tongue against the back of your upper teeth to prevent excess salivation.

Tip your head gently forward and cast your eyes downwards. This prevents too much excitement building up and distracting you from your mind.

Keep your eyes open, but not wide. Gaza down your nose towards the ground.

Ensure the shoulders remain level with the elbows and not pressed against your sides to allow airflow.

Vairochana's meditation posture also involves breathing techniques. This prepares our minds for the development of motivation and clears us of negative thoughts which could disrupt us. Think of it like this – we cannot see light through a dirty window until we clear the window of dirt. Until then, we cannot see clearly. This is the same with the mind when it comes to meditation – we cannot have a clear and free mind until we rid ourselves of negative thoughts and troubles which are holding us down. This can be accomplished by practicing breathing meditation.

Breathing Meditation

The purpose of breathing meditation: to calm the mind and develop your inner peace. This can be used alone if you don't have time to commit to a meditation session, but is most effective when coupled with physical meditation techniques.

Once in your meditation position, allow yourself to become aware of the thoughts and distractions that you have. Accept that they are there, otherwise you will not be able to understand and extinguish them. Calmly gracuate your attention towards your breathing. Let the rhythm stay calm and consistent, with deep and clear breaths. Imagine that you are breathing fresh and clean air that detoxifies your body of troubles; that flushes out negative thoughts in your head. Allow these thoughts to fade and vanish from yourself. Maintain this image, this visualisation, for 30 seconds or until the mind has reached a constant peaceful state. The more you concentrate on your breathing, the less able you will be to fixate on the negative thoughts and stressors in your mind.

Sit with your eyes partially closed and make sure your attention is on each and every inhale and exhale. Be strong. Feel the air rising up through your nostrils – appreciate the sensation of touch. Exclude everything else from your mind.

Be aware that, at first, you may feel as though your mind becomes cluttered with the silence – you aren't used to the process and the silence has caused your mind to fill it. But be patient. In reality, you are simply becoming aware of how busy your mind truly is. Continue to focus on your breathing. If you feel overwhelmed, slow you breathing down and take deeper breaths. Repeat this until you are in a peaceful state.

Mindfulness Meditation for Beginners

This is an adaption of many Buddhist meditation practices, but follows on from Vipassana meditation which will be discussed later. Mindfulness is the common goal of may Wester people who are interested in meditation and being introduced to the practice. Here, we can guide you to mindfulness through meditation.

Mindfulness meditation revolves around living in the present moment and blocking out all external stimuli – all sounds, smells, objects.

In practice, it is best to sit in position on a cushion with a straight and unsupported back. Be aware of your breathing. Focus on the present moment and don't add unnecessary tags to what it going on around you i.e. don't identify the smells you smell. Don't hear a bark and think 'dog', but merely 'sound'. Whatever stimuli surrounds you, calmly recognise what sense has been activated and return to a state of meditation. Do not let the distractions take you far from your state of peace.

This type of meditation can be easily implemented in to everyday life. When you are going for a walk or taking a break from work, calm your mind and limit your sense. Be present in that moment. This is perhaps the most recommended form of meditation to be introduced to and is the most popular for amongst young people in modern society due to how easy it can be to make a difference in our busy lives. Many people will only ever practice this type of meditation in their lifetimes.

Dharma: The Path of Buddha

The Buddhist path considers virtuous objects of meditation – anything that can cause our mind to become more calm and peaceful can be a virtuous object. This is the essence of objects in meditation. There are many objects which are neutral and cause us no response and thus cannot be an object of meditation – object that can will result in a positive or negative effect on our minds.

By relying on the spiritual guide that is Buddhism, we are practicing Dharma. Through these blessings we generate and feed our faith, our belief in the practice of meditation. We should follow the guidelines to reinforce this belief which, in turn, reinforces the results of meditation. We need to learn to appreciate our lives and realise the opportunities that present themselves to us in the practice of Dharma. To do so will inhibit us from engaging in meaningless thoughts and limiting our fulfilment in life. To do so leads to happiness. True happiness.

We should meditate on love for one another. On compassion and care for those around us, and those not. Our thoughts should be at one with all living beings – our aim is to eradicate the ignorance which shadows us all. With an honest heart, we can all achieve peace and spread it throughout modern society. Become a Buddha.

As we continue to meditate, our perception clears – the dirt on the glass washes away and all becomes clear. We will gain a deeper understanding of the reality that surrounds us. Our minds will transform on the path to enlightenment and mindfulness. When we internalise our realisation through meditation, the object can never again cause us sadness or anger.

Zazen: **Zen** Meditation

Zazen translated literally means 'Zen'. This is seated meditation in Japanese, much like what we have seen so far. This meditation traces back to the Indian monk Bodhidharma, but the most popular, Western adaption of Zen meditation originates from Dogen Zenji, the founder of Soto Zen Movement in Japan.

Zen meditation is traditionally performed on the floor with crossed legs, but can also be practices whilst sat upright on a chair. In terms of posture, it is very similar as that we have seen in the previous forms of meditation – straight back, gazing slightly down and still.

Zen meditation focusses largely on breathing. All attention should be on the movement of each breath going up through your nostrils. You can count these breaths in your mind to maintain a consistent pace of breath. Use these counts to remain focussed and keep your concentration.

This form of meditation requires no object to focus on, unlike Lamrim meditation. Zen meditation focusses purely on the moment, being aware of what passes through your mind at any one point in time without fixating on anything in particular. Your thought processes should be fluid and continuous.

Vipassana Meditation: The Meditation of Insight

Vipassana means insight; insight means Vipassana. Clear seeing is the focus of this traditional Buddhist practice and has become one of the most popular meditation practices in Western culture in recent years.

Most Vipassana meditations begin with breathing meditation as a preliminary stage to the practice as a means of creating an awareness. This should be achieved by following the general steps we have outlined so far. The focus will then shift towards developing mindfulness and insight.

Your attention must be focussed on the moment. Each and every sense you hold must be recognised – every sensation you feel, every smell and sounds. Feel the world around you passing through your senses. These are secondary objects that can be labelled i.e. sounds, smells. You should notice these, but only notice them. There is no need to identify what you are smelling or what you hear. Merely label these objects as 'smell' or 'sound'.

This will begin to transition towards feelings of your inner self – your emotions; your awareness of your own body. These are your primary objects and are the focus of this meditation.

As you practice this meditation, the sensations you recognise within you will develop an inner freedom and establish peace between your own body and the physical world that surrounds it.

Chapter 15: Boosting Your Self-Esteem

Are you aware of the current level of your self-esteem today? This is as important as knowing that you are alive. Self-esteem is defined as the way that you place value upon yourself, your abilities, and the way that people see you. High self-esteem could be manifested through various ways. These could include confidence, non-blaming attitude, optimism, ability to effectively manage and solve problems, awareness of limitations and abilities, self-care awareness, and the ability to stand up for one's decisions.

When self-esteem dips, it could be the ingredient to the loss of relationships, lack of confidence and overall incapability to deal with others effectively. Low self-esteem will debilitate your chances of realizing and using your full potentials.

Now, how will you know that your self-esteem is falling below the standard levels? Of course, there are a few very effective indicators of this condition. These are as follows:

Codependence(letting others make decisions for you)

Blaming type of behavior (self and others)

Negative outlook in life

Fear of taking risks even if there are promises of rewards.

Being perfectionist even in simple matters.

Inability to trust others (even those who are close to you)

Feelings of not being worthy of love and loving back.

Now, can you see why low self-esteem is deemed as destructive for you as a person? The signs of low self-esteem are more than enough to do this. Of course, this is something that you can work on. There is no need to seek professional help at this point in time. Low self-esteem is an easy obstacle that will be worth dealing with on your own.

If you want to quickly boost your self-esteem, there are actually 5 proven things that you can do. These include the following:

Recall your feelings when you were still trying to learn something new. Usually, you felt nervous, not confident about your capabilities to learn the said thing, and lost. By recalling these feelings, you will be reminded of the fact that it is included in the process of learning. If you are feeling down, take this moment as a new learning experience that could add up to a better you.

Work on something where you are skilled on or good at. You will be able to accomplish successes and the feeling of winning could push away the negative thoughts that you have.

Relax and do it seriously. You are not escaping from your problem, but just merely preparing yourself to deal with it. A massage, meditation, or simply lying down and listening to soft music can soothe your feelings and allow you to redirect your energy on taking away the sources of those negative thoughts.

Recall and count all of your achievements and wins all through life. Sit back and think of even those little things that gave you feelings of value and happiness. It will remind you that you are not as low as you are thinking right now.

Use the power of daily affirmations. What you say to yourself is very powerful. Your subconscious mind could easily pick up the idea behind the affirmations and condition your body to accomplish positive results.

Chapter 16: Self-Confident

Ok, if you've been following along so far and have done the exercises, you should have a pretty good feel for how this practice can benefit your everyday life. It will be slightly different, because you won't be roting the whole time during normal life. This chapter will give you some tips for using the element of mindfulness to elevate your life off the cushion.

I'm going to give you a tip right now that, although not a traditional mindfulness technique, will help give you a healthy energy when most needed. There are many times in life where you'll experience body sensations of nervousness. It might be before a big presentation or in times of uncertainty. Either way, always try to note it out. Since ultimately you can't escape your physiology, you may still be nervous. But you'll be more aware of the body sensations that make up nervousness. This is always the first step and after time, you'll come to regard the rising and falling of body sensations with less and less meaning. They are just sensations that come and go. More on that in the next book.

Once you can notice these body sensations, you might come to the realization that they are just sensations that the mind has associated with nervousness. This is how most of our experience is shaped. We had an experience a long time ago that our mind linked to danger and ever since then, whenever the mind suspects it's running into a similar experience it serves up the old panic sensation as a warning. The mind contributes to the feelings by labeling them as nervousness/anxiet and usually this labeling amplifies the experience. It's a maddening loop of mind and body.

Sometimes, just looking deeply at this experience is enough to break its hold. If it isn't and you're still feeling nervous that's Ok. This technique comes from cognitive psychology. Look at the feelings of nervousness and instead of labeling yourself as being "nervous," begin to think of the body sensations as "excitement." This has the amazing effect of short-circuiting the loop between the mind and the body.

This is made easier with your practice of being able to separate mind and body. We talked about this before; we often experience emotions as a lump of body and mind and then conceptualize what you're feeling with a word like anger, sadness, joy and so on.

With a little time and practice, you'll be able to transform the experience of nervousness into healthy excitement. You may even start to look forward to these feelings because of the reframing of what it means.

It may help to think about it this way. Take a few seconds and think about the feelings that you have in your body that you have come to represent nervousness. Now imagine that someone else can have the same exact body sensations and feel excitement or energy. The meaning our mind gives to the experience has a role in shaping the experience.

It may be clichéd to say that you can't control your circumstances, but you can control what you do with those circumstances, but in my experience this is totally true. The problem with that cliché and why people tend not to take it to heart is that no one ever tells you exactly how to control your reaction. The techniques in this book give you a great starting place to break the attachment to our conditicned responses and give you a little space to create a new response. Combine the noting technique with this tip on turning nervousness into excitement and you'll be well on your way to truly understanding the power of mindfulness.

Since nervousness and excitement are usually physiologically close in nature, this particular reframe is fairly easy to do successfully. With a little bit of experimentation and practice can you start to see how you might be able to apply this to turning insecurity into confidence? Feelings of weakness into feelings of strength? Or even anger into joy?

We will discuss this more in the next book, but I'll leave you with this tip. If you can't directly go from one emotion to another like you can with nervousness into excitement, then the trick is to physically manipulate some of the body sensations by finding some common point.

For instance, if you've just been cut off and you're really angry, those body sensations of anger probably aren't very close to joy. So you would start by noting the individual body sensations of anger. If after that they persist, then you want to start noticing feelings associated with joy. There is an energy or momentum usually to anger. It fires you up. People don't usually get sleepy when they're angry. Use this feeling of energy, since it has a common ground with joy or happiness, as the jumping off point to take you from one emotion to another. A feeling of energy can often be used to link one emotion to another.

Please experiment with this. It is a strong technique made even stronger with your newfound mindfulness practice.

While we're on the topic of creating body sensations, probably the most useful body sensation to create is love. Please stay with me for a bit. I promise this will be very pragmatic.

Love is a great feeling. Love for others as well as for yourself can have dramatic effects. Love is not something that has to happen when circumstances are just right, it's important to actively cultivate love — which will manifest itself in your actions and demeanor as being friendly, likeable and charismatic. People tend to like people who like them.

Again, there is no magic pill here. When I meditated with the monks, at the end of every session, we would end with what is called metta, or loving-kindness. This is not a practice that I would normally gravitate towards. But boy do I get up off the cushion feeling great after adding the loving-kindness to my practice.

The practice is simple. In a bit, I'll give you a few phrases you can use, but you can you make up anything you want, as long as it helps you to create the feelings of love.

In the beginning, it may be hard for you to "create" feelings. What I did when I first started doing this practice was to visualize my dog. Feelings of love would be generated all on their own. Using noting, I would note the feelings or just put my awareness on them. With just a little bit of intention, I would begin to have feelings of love welling up inside of me. With just that little spark, I would then let the body sensations well up inside to encompass me. Then I would imagine sending that love out to my family, friends, and the people in the room and eventually out to everyone on the planet.

Please note that I don't think that I was actually sending anything like energy out to the world. But the mind responds to the story you make up about what happens — so this useful visualization has a very real effect on you.

We used to say this after a meditation session:

May all beings be happy and well
May all beings be free from suffering, disease, grief, worry and illness
And be strong, self-confident, healthy and peaceful

You are free to use this or do your own search on the internet for something that resonates with you. As with the noting, it matters a lot less what you say then what the actual sensations are.

I recommend you incorporate this saying or one like it at the end of your mediation session. If it's hard to bring up the feelings, use someone like a parent or child or even a dog that you already love a lot and use that as a springboard to develop feelings of love and empathy for everyone. Yes, it's best if you let this particular practice expand to everyone, even people you don't like.

It's good to eventually use a phrase like the one above. I started by thinking of my dog, then letting it spread to myself and then eventually everyone. While holding that feeling, I would say the saying a couple of times. If you do that, what will eventually happen is you can lose the visualization and just say the saying. It will immediately bring up those feelings because you've linked the words with the feelings enough times. Like hearing a song on the radio that brings you back to the feelings you had about a person or a certain time in your life.

The metta phrase is a great little thing you should start to incorporate after every meditation session. I know it doesn't seem like much, but after you try it a few times I doubt you will ever abandon it.

You now have all the tools you need to greet every experience in live with excitement, enthusiasm and love.

Chapter 17: The Use Of Mindfulness In Today's World

Research into mindfulness largely began in the 1970's through the efforts of John Kabat-Zinn, the grandfather of mindfulness in American culture. Zinn is the founder of the Stress Reduction Clinic, located at the University of Massachusetts Medical School. Following his footsteps were individuals such as John Teasdale, Zindel Seagal, and Mark Williams.

Since the 1970's more than 1000 professional publications have published research on the medical and psychological benefits of mindfulness as well as its validity and the wide range of application. These benefits include the developing of greater awareness to habitual or automatic responses, leading to their

reduction or cessation. It includes the ability to respond more effectively to difficult or complex situations, the cultivation of greater clarity, and a greater sense balance in life.
Programs on Mindfulness

Mindfulness programs have been developed to teach mindfulness in a uniform and systematic to a growing market. The two main mindfulness programs that have been developed are Mindfulness-Based Stress Reduction (MBSR) and Mindfulness-Based Cognitive Therapy (MBCT). Both of these programs are experiential in their approach and consist of group sessions, home practice and a core curriculum that is taught by experienced teachers of mindfulness. Typically, they involve meeting two to three hours a week for eight weeks. Both programs have been successfully used as interventions by schools, hospitals, veteran agencies, and prisons. MBCT has been clinically approved in the United Kingdom as the preferred treatment for depression, while MBSR has been successfully used for people suffering from medical issues such as chronic pain. Both MBCT and MBSR are based on Buddhist principles minus any religious context.

Education

The educational sector is now beginning to provide mindfulness training to their staff and students.

Our schools face numerous challenges as they strive to educate our children. Reduced budgets, teacher turnover, and limited resources all have an impact on our children's ability to learn. Additionally, students today are bringing numerous challenges to the classroom, affecting both them and their teachers. Many forces come to bear, not the least of them being technology, the dynamics in the home, and challenged communities.

Conclusion

Hopefully you are excited to start living mindfully. You can get started today, there is no need to wait. You don't need any special equipment or any training. Just remember the three steps in mindful meditation:

Get Comfortable

Sit or lie down, stand or kneel, it doesn't matter what position you are in. Keep your back straight and get into any position that is comfortable to you. That is all you need to do to get started.

Pay Attention to Your Breath

Feel your breath. Feel it flowing into your body bringing life giving oxygen and feel it flowing back out again. You don't need to slow down your breathing or speed it up. Just let it flow.

Corral Your Thoughts

Don't give up when you feel your mind wander. Let your thoughts go for a moment. Don't chase them. Don't pay attention to them. But, every few breaths gently corral those thoughts and bring them back to your breath. Focus on your breath. And when those thoughts wander again let them go. Just bring them gently back to the breath. Keep doing this over and over. Eventually your thoughts won't wander so much and it will be easier to hold the focus on your breath.

These simple steps are the key to managing the terrible anxiety and other symptoms of PTSD, panic and anxiety disorders, depression and stress. You are ready now to take back your life, life in joy in the present moment, and live the life you were born to live.

www.ingramcontent.com/pod-product-compliance
Lightning Source LLC
Chambersburg PA
CBHW072004070526
44583CB00015B/1323